TEACHER'S PET PUBLICATIONS

PUZZLE PACK
for
Siddhartha

based on the book by
Hermann Hesse

Written by
Mary B. Collins

© 2008 Teacher's Pet Publications
All Rights Reserved

The materials in this packet are copyrighted
by Teacher's Pet Publications, Inc.

These pages may be duplicated by the purchaser
for use in the purchaser's own classroom.

Copying any of these materials and distributing them
for any other purpose is a violation of the copyright laws.

© 2008 Teacher's Pet Publications, Inc.
www.tpet.com

INTRODUCTION
If you already own the LitPlan for this title, this Puzzle Pack will refresh your Unit Resource Materials and Vocabulary Resource Materials sections plus give you additional materials you can substitute into the tests. If you do not already have a complete LitPlan, these pages will give you some supplemental materials to use with your own plan. There are two main groups of materials: one set for unit words (such as characters' names, symbols, places, etc.) and one set for vocabulary words associated with the book.

WORD LIST
There is a word list for both the unit words and the vocabulary words. These lists show you which words are being used in the materials and the clues or definitions being used for those words. You may want to give students a word list with clues/definitions to help them, or you may want students to only have a word list (without clues/definitions) if you want them to work a little harder. Both are available for duplication. The word lists can also be your "calling key" for the bingo games.

FILL IN THE BLANK AND MATCHING
There are 4 each of the fill in the blank and matching worksheets for both the unit and vocabulary words. These pages can be used either as extra worksheets for students or as objective parts of a unit test. They can be done individually if students need extra help or as a whole class activity to review the material covered.

MAGIC SQUARES
The magic squares not only reinforce the material covered but also work on reasoning and math skills. Many teachers have told us that their students really enjoy doing these!

WORD SEARCH PUZZLES
The word search words go in all directions, as indicated on your answer keys. Two of the word search puzzles have the clues listed rather than the words. This makes the puzzle a little more difficult, but it reinforces the material better. Two word search puzzles have words only for students who find the clue puzzles too difficult.

CROSSWORD PUZZLES
Both unit and vocabulary word sections have 4 crossword puzzles.

BINGO CARDS
There are 32 individual bingo cards for the unit words and 32 individual bingo cards for the vocabulary words. You can use your word list as a "call list," calling the words at random and marking them off of your list as you go, or you could use the flash cards by cutting them apart and drawing the words at random from a hat (or box or whatever). To make a better review, you might ask for the definition and spelling of each word as you call it out–or you could call out the definitions and have students tell you the words they need to look for on the puzzle.

JUGGLE LETTERS
The vocabulary juggle letter game is intended to help students learn the spellings of the words. One sheet has the definitions listed on it as an extra help for students who need it or to reinforce the definitions if you choose to do so.

FLASH CARDS
We've included a set of vocabulary flash cards you can duplicate, cut, and fold for your students. Some teachers make a few sets for general use by the class; others make a set for each student. Some teachers duplicate them for each student and have the students cut & fold their own. You can cut out just the words and put them in a hat, have each student pick out one word and write the definition and a sentence for that word. Students then swap words and papers, with the next student adding a sentence of his own under the last one. You can have students swap as many times as you like. Each time the student will read the sentences written prior to his own and then add a sentence. You can cut out the words and definitions separately and play "I Have; Who Has?" Each student in the room draws a word and definition. The first student says, "I have (the name of the word). Who has the definition?" The student with the definition reads it then says, "I have (the name of the vocabulary word she has). Who has the definition?" The round continues until all words and definitions have been given.

Siddhartha

No.	Word	Clue/Definition
1.	BIRD	Siddhartha dreamed that it died and he threw it away.
2.	BOAT	Siddhartha's son's means of escape
3.	BRAHMIN	Siddhartha's father is one.
4.	BUDDHA	He is recognized by his complete peacefulness.
5.	CLEVERNESS	Buddha warns Siddhartha about too much of this.
6.	DEATH	Siddhartha longs for it after leaving Kamala.
7.	DICE	Siddhartha became obsessed with this game.
8.	EXPERIENCE	Siddhartha believes he must gain this for himself.
9.	FATHER	Siddhartha saw him in his river reflection.
10.	FERRYMAN	Taught Siddhartha about the river
11.	FINDING	It means being receptive without a goal.
12.	GOTAMA	The Buddha
13.	GOVINDA	Faithful friend of Siddhartha since childhood
14.	HERON	One of the two animals Siddhartha associates himself with
15.	HYPNOTIZES	Siddhartha does this to the eldest Samana.
16.	JETAVANA	The Buddha was given this place in which to live.
17.	KAMALA	Courtesan who loved Siddhartha
18.	KAMASWAMI	Businessman who befriended Siddhartha
19.	KNOWLEDGE	Siddhartha's journey was to acquire this.
20.	LOVE	The Buddha forbade his followers to bind themselves to this.
21.	OM	Word-sound that brings Siddhartha a sense of peace
22.	RIVER	It symbolizes the flow of life.
23.	SAMANAS	Siddhartha and Govinda joined them.
24.	SEEKING	It means having a goal.
25.	SELF	Siddhartha desires to lose this.
26.	SIDDHARTHA	Son of a Brahmin who left home to find enlightenment
27.	SNAKE	It symbolizes the transformation of Siddhartha.
28.	SON	He steals a boat and runs away.
29.	STONE	Siddhartha tells Govinda that it could one day become a man.
30.	TEACHERS	Siddhartha lost the desire to have these.
31.	TIME	Secret from the river: there is no such thing as ___.
32.	TOWNSPEOPLE	They loved and admired Siddhartha.
33.	VASUDEVA	He taught Siddhartha about the river.
34.	WOODS	Where the Ferryman goes to die.

Siddhartha Fill In The Blanks 1

_____
_____
_____
_____
_____
_____
_____
_____
_____
_____
_____
_____
_____
_____
_____
_____
_____
_____
_____
_____

1. The Buddha forbade his followers to bind themselves to this.
2. Where the Ferryman goes to die.
3. Siddhartha saw him in his river reflection.
4. It symbolizes the transformation of Siddhartha.
5. Siddhartha believes he must gain this for himself.
6. They loved and admired Siddhartha.
7. Siddhartha longs for it after leaving Kamala.
8. The Buddha
9. Taught Siddhartha about the river
10. Siddhartha dreamed that it died and he threw it away.
11. Siddhartha lost the desire to have these.
12. Siddhartha and Govinda joined them.
13. The Buddha was given this place in which to live.
14. He taught Siddhartha about the river.
15. It means having a goal.
16. Siddhartha's father is one.
17. Faithful friend of Siddhartha since childhood
18. Siddhartha desires to lose this.
19. Courtesan who loved Siddhartha
20. Siddhartha's journey was to acquire this.

Siddhartha Fill In The Blanks 1 Answer Key

LOVE	1. The Buddha forbade his followers to bind themselves to this.
WOODS	2. Where the Ferryman goes to die.
FATHER	3. Siddhartha saw him in his river reflection.
SNAKE	4. It symbolizes the transformation of Siddhartha.
EXPERIENCE	5. Siddhartha believes he must gain this for himself.
TOWNSPEOPLE	6. They loved and admired Siddhartha.
DEATH	7. Siddhartha longs for it after leaving Kamala.
GOTAMA	8. The Buddha
FERRYMAN	9. Taught Siddhartha about the river
BIRD	10. Siddhartha dreamed that it died and he threw it away.
TEACHERS	11. Siddhartha lost the desire to have these.
SAMANAS	12. Siddhartha and Govinda joined them.
JETAVANA	13. The Buddha was given this place in which to live.
VASUDEVA	14. He taught Siddhartha about the river.
SEEKING	15. It means having a goal.
BRAHMIN	16. Siddhartha's father is one.
GOVINDA	17. Faithful friend of Siddhartha since childhood
SELF	18. Siddhartha desires to lose this.
KAMALA	19. Courtesan who loved Siddhartha
KNOWLEDGE	20. Siddhartha's journey was to acquire this.

Siddhartha Fill In The Blanks 2

_____

_____

_____

_____

_____

_____

_____

_____

_____

_____

_____

_____

_____

_____

_____

_____

_____

_____

_____

_____

1. Siddhartha desires to lose this.
2. Siddhartha became obsessed with this game.
3. Courtesan who loved Siddhartha
4. Secret from the river: there is no such thing as ___.
5. Siddhartha saw him in his river reflection.
6. Word-sound that brings Siddhartha a sense of peace
7. The Buddha forbade his followers to bind themselves to this.
8. He is recognized by his complete peacefulness.
9. Siddhartha lost the desire to have these.
10. Siddhartha dreamed that it died and he threw it away.
11. Siddhartha does this to the eldest Samana.
12. Siddhartha's journey was to acquire this.
13. Siddhartha's father is one.
14. He taught Siddhartha about the river.
15. He steals a boat and runs away.
16. The Buddha
17. Siddhartha believes he must gain this for himself.
18. Businessman who befriended Siddhartha
19. It means being receptive without a goal.
20. The Buddha was given this place in which to live.

Siddhartha Fill In The Blanks 2 Answer Key

SELF	1. Siddhartha desires to lose this.
DICE	2. Siddhartha became obsessed with this game.
KAMALA	3. Courtesan who loved Siddhartha
TIME	4. Secret from the river: there is no such thing as ___.
FATHER	5. Siddhartha saw him in his river reflection.
OM	6. Word-sound that brings Siddhartha a sense of peace
LOVE	7. The Buddha forbade his followers to bind themselves to this.
BUDDHA	8. He is recognized by his complete peacefulness.
TEACHERS	9. Siddhartha lost the desire to have these.
BIRD	10. Siddhartha dreamed that it died and he threw it away.
HYPNOTIZES	11. Siddhartha does this to the eldest Samana.
KNOWLEDGE	12. Siddhartha's journey was to acquire this.
BRAHMIN	13. Siddhartha's father is one.
VASUDEVA	14. He taught Siddhartha about the river.
SON	15. He steals a boat and runs away.
GOTAMA	16. The Buddha
EXPERIENCE	17. Siddhartha believes he must gain this for himself.
KAMASWAMI	18. Businessman who befriended Siddhartha
FINDING	19. It means being receptive without a goal.
JETAVANA	20. The Buddha was given this place in which to live.

Siddhartha Fill In The Blanks 3

_____

_____

_____

_____

_____

_____

_____

_____

_____

_____

_____

_____

_____

_____

_____

_____

_____

_____

_____

_____

1. Siddhartha desires to lose this.
2. He taught Siddhartha about the river.
3. They loved and admired Siddhartha.
4. Siddhartha longs for it after leaving Kamala.
5. Siddhartha dreamed that it died and he threw it away.
6. The Buddha
7. It symbolizes the transformation of Siddhartha.
8. Son of a Brahmin who left home to find enlightenment
9. He is recognized by his complete peacefulness.
10. Siddhartha does this to the eldest Samana.
11. It means being receptive without a goal.
12. Buddha warns Siddhartha about too much of this.
13. Siddhartha saw him in his river reflection.
14. Word-sound that brings Siddhartha a sense of peace
15. The Buddha forbade his followers to bind themselves to this.
16. Taught Siddhartha about the river
17. Siddhartha tells Govinda that it could one day become a man.
18. Faithful friend of Siddhartha since childhood
19. Siddhartha's son's means of escape
20. Siddhartha's father is one.

Siddhartha Fill In The Blanks 3 Answer Key

SELF	1. Siddhartha desires to lose this.
VASUDEVA	2. He taught Siddhartha about the river.
TOWNSPEOPLE	3. They loved and admired Siddhartha.
DEATH	4. Siddhartha longs for it after leaving Kamala.
BIRD	5. Siddhartha dreamed that it died and he threw it away.
GOTAMA	6. The Buddha
SNAKE	7. It symbolizes the transformation of Siddhartha.
SIDDHARTHA	8. Son of a Brahmin who left home to find enlightenment
BUDDHA	9. He is recognized by his complete peacefulness.
HYPNOTIZES	10. Siddhartha does this to the eldest Samana.
FINDING	11. It means being receptive without a goal.
CLEVERNESS	12. Buddha warns Siddhartha about too much of this.
FATHER	13. Siddhartha saw him in his river reflection.
OM	14. Word-sound that brings Siddhartha a sense of peace
LOVE	15. The Buddha forbade his followers to bind themselves to this.
FERRYMAN	16. Taught Siddhartha about the river
STONE	17. Siddhartha tells Govinda that it could one day become a man.
GOVINDA	18. Faithful friend of Siddhartha since childhood
BOAT	19. Siddhartha's son's means of escape
BRAHMIN	20. Siddhartha's father is one.

Siddhartha Fill In The Blanks 4

_____

_____

_____

_____

_____

_____

_____

_____

_____

_____

_____

_____

_____

_____

_____

_____

_____

_____

_____

_____

1. It means having a goal.
2. Taught Siddhartha about the river
3. Buddha warns Siddhartha about too much of this.
4. Siddhartha desires to lose this.
5. It symbolizes the flow of life.
6. Where the Ferryman goes to die.
7. Siddhartha lost the desire to have these.
8. Businessman who befriended Siddhartha
9. One of the two animals Siddhartha associates himself with
10. Courtesan who loved Siddhartha
11. Siddhartha's journey was to acquire this.
12. Siddhartha and Govinda joined them.
13. Siddhartha's father is one.
14. Siddhartha tells Govinda that it could one day become a man.
15. Siddhartha believes he must gain this for himself.
16. Faithful friend of Siddhartha since childhood
17. He is recognized by his complete peacefulness.
18. Word-sound that brings Siddhartha a sense of peace
19. Siddhartha does this to the eldest Samana.
20. Siddhartha saw him in his river reflection.

Siddhartha Fill In The Blanks 4 Answer Key

SEEKING	1. It means having a goal.
FERRYMAN	2. Taught Siddhartha about the river
CLEVERNESS	3. Buddha warns Siddhartha about too much of this.
SELF	4. Siddhartha desires to lose this.
RIVER	5. It symbolizes the flow of life.
WOODS	6. Where the Ferryman goes to die.
TEACHERS	7. Siddhartha lost the desire to have these.
KAMASWAMI	8. Businessman who befriended Siddhartha
HERON	9. One of the two animals Siddhartha associates himself with
KAMALA	10. Courtesan who loved Siddhartha
KNOWLEDGE	11. Siddhartha's journey was to acquire this.
SAMANAS	12. Siddhartha and Govinda joined them.
BRAHMIN	13. Siddhartha's father is one.
STONE	14. Siddhartha tells Govinda that it could one day become a man.
EXPERIENCE	15. Siddhartha believes he must gain this for himself.
GOVINDA	16. Faithful friend of Siddhartha since childhood
BUDDHA	17. He is recognized by his complete peacefulness.
OM	18. Word-sound that brings Siddhartha a sense of peace
HYPNOTIZES	19. Siddhartha does this to the eldest Samana.
FATHER	20. Siddhartha saw him in his river reflection.

Siddhartha Matching 1

___ 1. STONE
___ 2. DEATH
___ 3. TOWNSPEOPLE
___ 4. HYPNOTIZES
___ 5. EXPERIENCE
___ 6. FATHER
___ 7. SNAKE
___ 8. LOVE
___ 9. SON
___ 10. SIDDHARTHA
___ 11. BOAT
___ 12. SEEKING
___ 13. SAMANAS
___ 14. KNOWLEDGE
___ 15. BRAHMIN
___ 16. WOODS
___ 17. GOTAMA
___ 18. HERON
___ 19. TIME
___ 20. VASUDEVA
___ 21. OM
___ 22. JETAVANA
___ 23. KAMALA
___ 24. DICE
___ 25. FINDING

A. He taught Siddhartha about the river.
B. Siddhartha and Govinda joined them.
C. Courtesan who loved Siddhartha
D. It means being receptive without a goal.
E. The Buddha was given this place in which to live.
F. The Buddha
G. Siddhartha does this to the eldest Samana.
H. It means having a goal.
I. Son of a Brahmin who left home to find enlightenment
J. Siddhartha tells Govinda that it could one day become a man.
K. Siddhartha's son's means of escape
L. Where the Ferryman goes to die.
M. Siddhartha's journey was to acquire this.
N. Word-sound that brings Siddhartha a sense of peace
O. Secret from the river: there is no such thing as ___.
P. They loved and admired Siddhartha.
Q. Siddhartha saw him in his river reflection.
R. It symbolizes the transformation of Siddhartha.
S. Siddhartha became obsessed with this game.
T. The Buddha forbade his followers to bind themselves to this.
U. Siddhartha's father is one.
V. Siddhartha longs for it after leaving Kamala.
W. Siddhartha believes he must gain this for himself.
X. He steals a boat and runs away.
Y. One of the two animals Siddhartha associates himself with

Siddhartha Matching 1 Answer Key

J - 1. STONE	A.	He taught Siddhartha about the river.
V - 2. DEATH	B.	Siddhartha and Govinda joined them.
P - 3. TOWNSPEOPLE	C.	Courtesan who loved Siddhartha
G - 4. HYPNOTIZES	D.	It means being receptive without a goal.
W - 5. EXPERIENCE	E.	The Buddha was given this place in which to live.
Q - 6. FATHER	F.	The Buddha
R - 7. SNAKE	G.	Siddhartha does this to the eldest Samana.
T - 8. LOVE	H.	It means having a goal.
X - 9. SON	I.	Son of a Brahmin who left home to find enlightenment
I - 10. SIDDHARTHA	J.	Siddhartha tells Govinda that it could one day become a man.
K - 11. BOAT	K.	Siddhartha's son's means of escape
H - 12. SEEKING	L.	Where the Ferryman goes to die.
B - 13. SAMANAS	M.	Siddhartha's journey was to acquire this.
M - 14. KNOWLEDGE	N.	Word-sound that brings Siddhartha a sense of peace
U - 15. BRAHMIN	O.	Secret from the river: there is no such thing as ___.
L - 16. WOODS	P.	They loved and admired Siddhartha.
F - 17. GOTAMA	Q.	Siddhartha saw him in his river reflection.
Y - 18. HERON	R.	It symbolizes the transformation of Siddhartha.
O - 19. TIME	S.	Siddhartha became obsessed with this game.
A - 20. VASUDEVA	T.	The Buddha forbade his followers to bind themselves to this.
N - 21. OM	U.	Siddhartha's father is one.
E - 22. JETAVANA	V.	Siddhartha longs for it after leaving Kamala.
C - 23. KAMALA	W.	Siddhartha believes he must gain this for himself.
S - 24. DICE	X.	He steals a boat and runs away.
D - 25. FINDING	Y.	One of the two animals Siddhartha associates himself with

Siddhartha Matching 2

___ 1. LOVE
___ 2. STONE
___ 3. RIVER
___ 4. BRAHMIN
___ 5. SON
___ 6. TEACHERS
___ 7. SELF
___ 8. VASUDEVA
___ 9. BOAT
___ 10. SIDDHARTHA
___ 11. FATHER
___ 12. SEEKING
___ 13. KAMASWAMI
___ 14. FERRYMAN
___ 15. HERON
___ 16. KNOWLEDGE
___ 17. GOTAMA
___ 18. OM
___ 19. TOWNSPEOPLE
___ 20. WOODS
___ 21. BUDDHA
___ 22. CLEVERNESS
___ 23. GOVINDA
___ 24. HYPNOTIZES
___ 25. BIRD

A. Siddhartha lost the desire to have these.
B. The Buddha
C. He taught Siddhartha about the river.
D. He steals a boat and runs away.
E. Siddhartha does this to the eldest Samana.
F. Taught Siddhartha about the river
G. It symbolizes the flow of life.
H. Siddhartha's father is one.
I. Siddhartha tells Govinda that it could one day become a man.
J. Faithful friend of Siddhartha since childhood
K. Where the Ferryman goes to die.
L. Siddhartha desires to lose this.
M. Buddha warns Siddhartha about too much of this.
N. He is recognized by his complete peacefulness.
O. The Buddha forbade his followers to bind themselves to this.
P. They loved and admired Siddhartha.
Q. Siddhartha saw him in his river reflection.
R. Siddhartha's son's means of escape
S. Siddhartha's journey was to acquire this.
T. One of the two animals Siddhartha associates himself with
U. It means having a goal.
V. Word-sound that brings Siddhartha a sense of peace
W. Son of a Brahmin who left home to find enlightenment
X. Businessman who befriended Siddhartha
Y. Siddhartha dreamed that it died and he threw it away.

Siddhartha Matching 2 Answer Key

O - 1.	LOVE	A. Siddhartha lost the desire to have these.
I - 2.	STONE	B. The Buddha
G - 3.	RIVER	C. He taught Siddhartha about the river.
H - 4.	BRAHMIN	D. He steals a boat and runs away.
D - 5.	SON	E. Siddhartha does this to the eldest Samana.
A - 6.	TEACHERS	F. Taught Siddhartha about the river
L - 7.	SELF	G. It symbolizes the flow of life.
C - 8.	VASUDEVA	H. Siddhartha's father is one.
R - 9.	BOAT	I. Siddhartha tells Govinda that it could one day become a man.
W - 10.	SIDDHARTHA	J. Faithful friend of Siddhartha since childhood
Q - 11.	FATHER	K. Where the Ferryman goes to die.
U - 12.	SEEKING	L. Siddhartha desires to lose this.
X - 13.	KAMASWAMI	M. Buddha warns Siddhartha about too much of this.
F - 14.	FERRYMAN	N. He is recognized by his complete peacefulness.
T - 15.	HERON	O. The Buddha forbade his followers to bind themselves to this.
S - 16.	KNOWLEDGE	P. They loved and admired Siddhartha.
B - 17.	GOTAMA	Q. Siddhartha saw him in his river reflection.
V - 18.	OM	R. Siddhartha's son's means of escape
P - 19.	TOWNSPEOPLE	S. Siddhartha's journey was to acquire this.
K - 20.	WOODS	T. One of the two animals Siddhartha associates himself with
N - 21.	BUDDHA	U. It means having a goal.
M - 22.	CLEVERNESS	V. Word-sound that brings Siddhartha a sense of peace
J - 23.	GOVINDA	W. Son of a Brahmin who left home to find enlightenment
E - 24.	HYPNOTIZES	X. Businessman who befriended Siddhartha
Y - 25.	BIRD	Y. Siddhartha dreamed that it died and he threw it away.

Siddhartha Matching 3

___ 1. SIDDHARTHA
___ 2. KAMALA
___ 3. EXPERIENCE
___ 4. OM
___ 5. RIVER
___ 6. SNAKE
___ 7. VASUDEVA
___ 8. SEEKING
___ 9. TIME
___ 10. CLEVERNESS
___ 11. KAMASWAMI
___ 12. BOAT
___ 13. BRAHMIN
___ 14. JETAVANA
___ 15. STONE
___ 16. GOTAMA
___ 17. SAMANAS
___ 18. HERON
___ 19. WOODS
___ 20. HYPNOTIZES
___ 21. SON
___ 22. TEACHERS
___ 23. BIRD
___ 24. FINDING
___ 25. DICE

A. One of the two animals Siddhartha associates himself with
B. Siddhartha dreamed that it died and he threw it away.
C. It symbolizes the transformation of Siddhartha.
D. It means having a goal.
E. Courtesan who loved Siddhartha
F. It means being receptive without a goal.
G. Siddhartha lost the desire to have these.
H. Businessman who befriended Siddhartha
I. Siddhartha's father is one.
J. Siddhartha does this to the eldest Samana.
K. He taught Siddhartha about the river.
L. He steals a boat and runs away.
M. It symbolizes the flow of life.
N. The Buddha was given this place in which to live.
O. Secret from the river: there is no such thing as ___.
P. Siddhartha's son's means of escape
Q. Where the Ferryman goes to die.
R. Siddhartha became obsessed with this game.
S. Siddhartha tells Govinda that it could one day become a man.
T. The Buddha
U. Son of a Brahmin who left home to find enlightenment
V. Siddhartha and Govinda joined them.
W. Word-sound that brings Siddhartha a sense of peace
X. Buddha warns Siddhartha about too much of this.
Y. Siddhartha believes he must gain this for himself.

Siddhartha Matching 3 Answer Key

U - 1. SIDDHARTHA	A.	One of the two animals Siddhartha associates himself with
E - 2. KAMALA	B.	Siddhartha dreamed that it died and he threw it away.
Y - 3. EXPERIENCE	C.	It symbolizes the transformation of Siddhartha.
W - 4. OM	D.	It means having a goal.
M - 5. RIVER	E.	Courtesan who loved Siddhartha
C - 6. SNAKE	F.	It means being receptive without a goal.
K - 7. VASUDEVA	G.	Siddhartha lost the desire to have these.
D - 8. SEEKING	H.	Businessman who befriended Siddhartha
O - 9. TIME	I.	Siddhartha's father is one.
X - 10. CLEVERNESS	J.	Siddhartha does this to the eldest Samana.
H - 11. KAMASWAMI	K.	He taught Siddhartha about the river.
P - 12. BOAT	L.	He steals a boat and runs away.
I - 13. BRAHMIN	M.	It symbolizes the flow of life.
N - 14. JETAVANA	N.	The Buddha was given this place in which to live.
S - 15. STONE	O.	Secret from the river: there is no such thing as ___.
T - 16. GOTAMA	P.	Siddhartha's son's means of escape
V - 17. SAMANAS	Q.	Where the Ferryman goes to die.
A - 18. HERON	R.	Siddhartha became obsessed with this game.
Q - 19. WOODS	S.	Siddhartha tells Govinda that it could one day become a man.
J - 20. HYPNOTIZES	T.	The Buddha
L - 21. SON	U.	Son of a Brahmin who left home to find enlightenment
G - 22. TEACHERS	V.	Siddhartha and Govinda joined them.
B - 23. BIRD	W.	Word-sound that brings Siddhartha a sense of peace
F - 24. FINDING	X.	Buddha warns Siddhartha about too much of this.
R - 25. DICE	Y.	Siddhartha believes he must gain this for himself.

Siddhartha Matching 4

___ 1. FINDING
___ 2. DICE
___ 3. TIME
___ 4. BIRD
___ 5. SEEKING
___ 6. HERON
___ 7. TEACHERS
___ 8. GOTAMA
___ 9. SIDDHARTHA
___10. FATHER
___11. SNAKE
___12. SAMANAS
___13. CLEVERNESS
___14. TOWNSPEOPLE
___15. FERRYMAN
___16. HYPNOTIZES
___17. SON
___18. OM
___19. JETAVANA
___20. KNOWLEDGE
___21. BRAHMIN
___22. LOVE
___23. SELF
___24. DEATH
___25. KAMALA

A. Secret from the river: there is no such thing as ___.
B. He steals a boat and runs away.
C. Siddhartha desires to lose this.
D. It means having a goal.
E. It symbolizes the transformation of Siddhartha.
F. They loved and admired Siddhartha.
G. Siddhartha longs for it after leaving Kamala.
H. Siddhartha and Govinda joined them.
I. Siddhartha does this to the eldest Samana.
J. It means being receptive without a goal.
K. One of the two animals Siddhartha associates himself with
L. The Buddha forbade his followers to bind themselves to this.
M. Courtesan who loved Siddhartha
N. The Buddha was given this place in which to live.
O. Siddhartha lost the desire to have these.
P. Taught Siddhartha about the river
Q. Son of a Brahmin who left home to find enlightenment
R. Siddhartha saw him in his river reflection.
S. Buddha warns Siddhartha about too much of this.
T. Siddhartha dreamed that it died and he threw it away.
U. Siddhartha became obsessed with this game.
V. Siddhartha's father is one.
W. The Buddha
X. Word-sound that brings Siddhartha a sense of peace
Y. Siddhartha's journey was to acquire this.

Siddhartha Matching 4 Answer Key

- J - 1. FINDING
- U - 2. DICE
- A - 3. TIME
- T - 4. BIRD
- D - 5. SEEKING
- K - 6. HERON
- O - 7. TEACHERS
- W - 8. GOTAMA
- Q - 9. SIDDHARTHA
- R - 10. FATHER
- E - 11. SNAKE
- H - 12. SAMANAS
- S - 13. CLEVERNESS
- F - 14. TOWNSPEOPLE
- P - 15. FERRYMAN
- I - 16. HYPNOTIZES
- B - 17. SON
- X - 18. OM
- N - 19. JETAVANA
- Y - 20. KNOWLEDGE
- V - 21. BRAHMIN
- L - 22. LOVE
- C - 23. SELF
- G - 24. DEATH
- M - 25. KAMALA

A. Secret from the river: there is no such thing as ___.
B. He steals a boat and runs away.
C. Siddhartha desires to lose this.
D. It means having a goal.
E. It symbolizes the transformation of Siddhartha.
F. They loved and admired Siddhartha.
G. Siddhartha longs for it after leaving Kamala.
H. Siddhartha and Govinda joined them.
I. Siddhartha does this to the eldest Samana.
J. It means being receptive without a goal.
K. One of the two animals Siddhartha associates himself with
L. The Buddha forbade his followers to bind themselves to this.
M. Courtesan who loved Siddhartha
N. The Buddha was given this place in which to live.
O. Siddhartha lost the desire to have these.
P. Taught Siddhartha about the river
Q. Son of a Brahmin who left home to find enlightenment
R. Siddhartha saw him in his river reflection.
S. Buddha warns Siddhartha about too much of this.
T. Siddhartha dreamed that it died and he threw it away.
U. Siddhartha became obsessed with this game.
V. Siddhartha's father is one.
W. The Buddha
X. Word-sound that brings Siddhartha a sense of peace
Y. Siddhartha's journey was to acquire this.

Siddhartha Magic Squares 1

Match the definition with the vocabulary word. Put your answers in the magic squares below. When your answers are correct, all columns and rows will add to the same number.

A. TEACHERS
B. DEATH
C. OM
D. SEEKING
E. CLEVERNESS
F. FERRYMAN
G. SON
H. FATHER
I. LOVE
J. SELF
K. KAMALA
L. DICE
M. WOODS
N. GOTAMA
O. HERON
P. BUDDHA

1. Siddhartha longs for it after leaving Kamala.
2. He steals a boat and runs away.
3. Courtesan who loved Siddhartha
4. The Buddha
5. Where the Ferryman goes to die.
6. Siddhartha became obsessed with this game.
7. Siddhartha saw him in his river reflection.
8. Siddhartha lost the desire to have these.
9. He is recognized by his complete peacefulness.
10. The Buddha forbade his followers to bind themselves to this.
11. Buddha warns Siddhartha about too much of this.
12. It means having a goal.
13. Word-sound that brings Siddhartha a sense of peace
14. Taught Siddhartha about the river
15. Siddhartha desires to lose this.
16. One of the two animals Siddhartha associates himself with

A=	B=	C=	D=
E=	F=	G=	H=
I=	J=	K=	L=
M=	N=	O=	P=

Siddhartha Magic Squares 1 Answer Key

Match the definition with the vocabulary word. Put your answers in the magic squares below. When your answers are correct, all columns and rows will add to the same number.

A. TEACHERS
B. DEATH
C. OM
D. SEEKING
E. CLEVERNESS
F. FERRYMAN
G. SON
H. FATHER
I. LOVE
J. SELF
K. KAMALA
L. DICE
M. WOODS
N. GOTAMA
O. HERON
P. BUDDHA

1. Siddhartha longs for it after leaving Kamala.
2. He steals a boat and runs away.
3. Courtesan who loved Siddhartha
4. The Buddha
5. Where the Ferryman goes to die.
6. Siddhartha became obsessed with this game.
7. Siddhartha saw him in his river reflection.
8. Siddhartha lost the desire to have these.
9. He is recognized by his complete peacefulness.
10. The Buddha forbade his followers to bind themselves to this.
11. Buddha warns Siddhartha about too much of this.
12. It means having a goal.
13. Word-sound that brings Siddhartha a sense of peace
14. Taught Siddhartha about the river
15. Siddhartha desires to lose this.
16. One of the two animals Siddhartha associates himself with

A=8	B=1	C=13	D=12
E=11	F=14	G=2	H=7
I=10	J=15	K=3	L=6
M=5	N=4	O=16	P=9

Siddhartha Magic Squares 2

Match the definition with the vocabulary word. Put your answers in the magic squares below. When your answers are correct, all columns and rows will add to the same number.

A. FATHER
B. TEACHERS
C. SAMANAS
D. HERON
E. JETAVANA
F. HYPNOTIZES
G. LOVE
H. KAMALA
I. OM
J. BUDDHA
K. SIDDHARTHA
L. GOTAMA
M. DICE
N. BIRD
O. DEATH
P. EXPERIENCE

1. Siddhartha does this to the eldest Samana.
2. Word-sound that brings Siddhartha a sense of peace
3. Siddhartha longs for it after leaving Kamala.
4. One of the two animals Siddhartha associates himself with
5. Siddhartha became obsessed with this game.
6. Siddhartha lost the desire to have these.
7. Courtesan who loved Siddhartha
8. Son of a Brahmin who left home to find enlightenment
9. Siddhartha and Govinda joined them.
10. Siddhartha believes he must gain this for himself.
11. He is recognized by his complete peacefulness.
12. The Buddha was given this place in which to live.
13. The Buddha
14. The Buddha forbade his followers to bind themselves to this.
15. Siddhartha saw him in his river reflection.
16. Siddhartha dreamed that it died and he threw it away.

A=	B=	C=	D=
E=	F=	G=	H=
I=	J=	K=	L=
M=	N=	O=	P=

Siddhartha Magic Squares 2 Answer Key

Match the definition with the vocabulary word. Put your answers in the magic squares below. When your answers are correct, all columns and rows will add to the same number.

A. FATHER
B. TEACHERS
C. SAMANAS
D. HERON
E. JETAVANA
F. HYPNOTIZES
G. LOVE
H. KAMALA
I. OM
J. BUDDHA
K. SIDDHARTHA
L. GOTAMA
M. DICE
N. BIRD
O. DEATH
P. EXPERIENCE

1. Siddhartha does this to the eldest Samana.
2. Word-sound that brings Siddhartha a sense of peace
3. Siddhartha longs for it after leaving Kamala.
4. One of the two animals Siddhartha associates himself with
5. Siddhartha became obsessed with this game.
6. Siddhartha lost the desire to have these.
7. Courtesan who loved Siddhartha
8. Son of a Brahmin who left home to find enlightenment
9. Siddhartha and Govinda joined them.
10. Siddhartha believes he must gain this for himself.
11. He is recognized by his complete peacefulness.
12. The Buddha was given this place in which to live.
13. The Buddha
14. The Buddha forbade his followers to bind themselves to this.
15. Siddhartha saw him in his river reflection.
16. Siddhartha dreamed that it died and he threw it away.

A=15	B=6	C=9	D=4
E=12	F=1	G=14	H=7
I=2	J=11	K=8	L=13
M=5	N=16	O=3	P=10

Siddhartha Magic Squares 3

Match the definition with the vocabulary word. Put your answers in the magic squares below. When your answers are correct, all columns and rows will add to the same number.

A. RIVER
B. SIDDHARTHA
C. TIME
D. LOVE
E. GOVINDA
F. BRAHMIN
G. FATHER
H. TOWNSPEOPLE
I. TEACHERS
J. BIRD
K. SON
L. KNOWLEDGE
M. HERON
N. EXPERIENCE
O. BUDDHA
P. VASUDEVA

1. He is recognized by his complete peacefulness.
2. Siddhartha dreamed that it died and he threw it away.
3. They loved and admired Siddhartha.
4. It symbolizes the flow of life.
5. The Buddha forbade his followers to bind themselves to this.
6. Faithful friend of Siddhartha since childhood
7. He steals a boat and runs away.
8. Siddhartha believes he must gain this for himself.
9. Siddhartha's father is one.
10. Secret from the river: there is no such thing as ___.
11. One of the two animals Siddhartha associates himself with
12. Siddhartha's journey was to acquire this.
13. Siddhartha lost the desire to have these.
14. He taught Siddhartha about the river.
15. Son of a Brahmin who left home to find enlightenment
16. Siddhartha saw him in his river reflection.

A= 4	B= 15	C= 10	D= 5
E= 6	F= 9	G= 16	H= 3
I= 13	J= 2	K= 7	L= 12
M= 11	N= 8	O= 1	P= 14

Siddhartha Magic Squares 3 Answer Key

Match the definition with the vocabulary word. Put your answers in the magic squares below. When your answers are correct, all columns and rows will add to the same number.

A. RIVER
B. SIDDHARTHA
C. TIME
D. LOVE
E. GOVINDA
F. BRAHMIN
G. FATHER
H. TOWNSPEOPLE
I. TEACHERS
J. BIRD
K. SON
L. KNOWLEDGE
M. HERON
N. EXPERIENCE
O. BUDDHA
P. VASUDEVA

1. He is recognized by his complete peacefulness.
2. Siddhartha dreamed that it died and he threw it away.
3. They loved and admired Siddhartha.
4. It symbolizes the flow of life.
5. The Buddha forbade his followers to bind themselves to this.
6. Faithful friend of Siddhartha since childhood
7. He steals a boat and runs away.
8. Siddhartha believes he must gain this for himself.
9. Siddhartha's father is one.
10. Secret from the river: there is no such thing as ___.
11. One of the two animals Siddhartha associates himself with
12. Siddhartha's journey was to acquire this.
13. Siddhartha lost the desire to have these.
14. He taught Siddhartha about the river.
15. Son of a Brahmin who left home to find enlightenment
16. Siddhartha saw him in his river reflection.

A=4	B=15	C=10	D=5
E=6	F=9	G=16	H=3
I=13	J=2	K=7	L=12
M=11	N=8	O=1	P=14

Siddhartha Magic Squares 4

Match the definition with the vocabulary word. Put your answers in the magic squares below. When your answers are correct, all columns and rows will add to the same number.

A. FERRYMAN
B. SNAKE
C. SON
D. WOODS
E. KAMASWAMI
F. SIDDHARTHA
G. FATHER
H. SELF
I. FINDING
J. TIME
K. BRAHMIN
L. TOWNSPEOPLE
M. TEACHERS
N. KAMALA
O. STONE
P. SAMANAS

1. Siddhartha lost the desire to have these.
2. Son of a Brahmin who left home to find enlightenment
3. Siddhartha desires to lose this.
4. Siddhartha tells Govinda that it could one day become a man.
5. They loved and admired Siddhartha.
6. He steals a boat and runs away.
7. Taught Siddhartha about the river.
8. Secret from the river: there is no such thing as ___.
9. Siddhartha's father is one.
10. Where the Ferryman goes to die.
11. It symbolizes the transformation of Siddhartha.
12. It means being receptive without a goal.
13. Courtesan who loved Siddhartha
14. Businessman who befriended Siddhartha
15. Siddhartha saw him in his river reflection.
16. Siddhartha and Govinda joined them.

A=	B=	C=	D=
E=	F=	G=	H=
I=	J=	K=	L=
M=	N=	O=	P=

Siddhartha Magic Squares 4 Answer Key

Match the definition with the vocabulary word. Put your answers in the magic squares below. When your answers are correct, all columns and rows will add to the same number.

A. FERRYMAN
B. SNAKE
C. SON
D. WOODS
E. KAMASWAMI
F. SIDDHARTHA
G. FATHER
H. SELF
I. FINDING
J. TIME
K. BRAHMIN
L. TOWNSPEOPLE
M. TEACHERS
N. KAMALA
O. STONE
P. SAMANAS

1. Siddhartha lost the desire to have these.
2. Son of a Brahmin who left home to find enlightenment
3. Siddhartha desires to lose this.
4. Siddhartha tells Govinda that it could one day become a man.
5. They loved and admired Siddhartha.
6. He steals a boat and runs away.
7. Taught Siddhartha about the river
8. Secret from the river: there is no such thing as ___.
9. Siddhartha's father is one.
10. Where the Ferryman goes to die.
11. It symbolizes the transformation of Siddhartha.
12. It means being receptive without a goal.
13. Courtesan who loved Siddhartha
14. Businessman who befriended Siddhartha
15. Siddhartha saw him in his river reflection.
16. Siddhartha and Govinda joined them.

A=7	B=11	C=6	D=10
E=14	F=2	G=15	H=3
I=12	J=8	K=9	L=5
M=1	N=13	O=4	P=16

Siddhartha Word Search 1

```
R I V E R K N O W L E D G E D M H X B R
B G J K W P R D D J S M R J W M E Y R D
P Y E K A B S S E N R E V E L C R G A Q
J S T A T M K T P M J X E G G R O N H G
W F A M T B A Z T P N T S K Y J N Z M Q
J Y V A B O T L N D A B D A I S B G I W
G G A S V L W J A W M D Q T M N H M N K
D B N W B J B N M Y Y C B H D A G N G F
C T A A G H J S S E R W N I B H N N V J
K C X M D S S O C P R T R L R D I A A J
G O V I N D A N E R E H T A F D L D S D
N Z C A O M E V F A F O M B N U V E U R
S E K O B I O L C Y T A P I K B L A D Z
H E W G R L G H E T T I F L M F X T E K
G R Q E H L E N A O M K M O E G W H V B
K C P F M R O O G M C X C E Z H C X A D
K X V D S T B H Y P N O T I Z E S Q L W
E D Z H S I D D H A R T H A J D Z T V L
```

Buddha warns Siddhartha about too much of this. (10)
Businessman who befriended Siddhartha (9)
Courtesan who loved Siddhartha (6)
Faithful friend of Siddhartha since childhood (7)
He is recognized by his complete peacefulness. (6)
He steals a boat and runs away. (3)
He taught Siddhartha about the river. (8)
It means being receptive without a goal. (7)
It means having a goal. (7)
It symbolizes the flow of life. (5)
It symbolizes the transformation of Siddhartha. (5)
One of the two animals Siddhartha associates himself with (5)
Secret from the river: there is no such thing as ___. (4)
Siddhartha and Govinda joined them. (7)
Siddhartha became obsessed with this game. (4)
Siddhartha believes he must gain this for himself. (10)
Siddhartha desires to lose this. (4)
Siddhartha does this to the eldest Samana. (10)
Siddhartha dreamed that it died and he threw it away. (4)
Siddhartha longs for it after leaving Kamala. (5)
Siddhartha lost the desire to have these. (8)
Siddhartha saw him in his river reflection. (6)
Siddhartha tells Govinda that it could one day become a man. (5)
Siddhartha's father is one. (7)
Siddhartha's journey was to acquire this. (9)
Siddhartha's son's means of escape (4)
Son of a Brahmin who left home to find enlightenment (10)
Taught Siddhartha about the river (8)
The Buddha (6)
The Buddha forbade his followers to bind themselves to this. (4)
The Buddha was given this place in which to live. (8)
They loved and admired Siddhartha. (11)
Where the Ferryman goes to die. (5)
Word-sound that brings Siddhartha a sense of peace (2)

Siddhartha Word Search 1 Answer Key

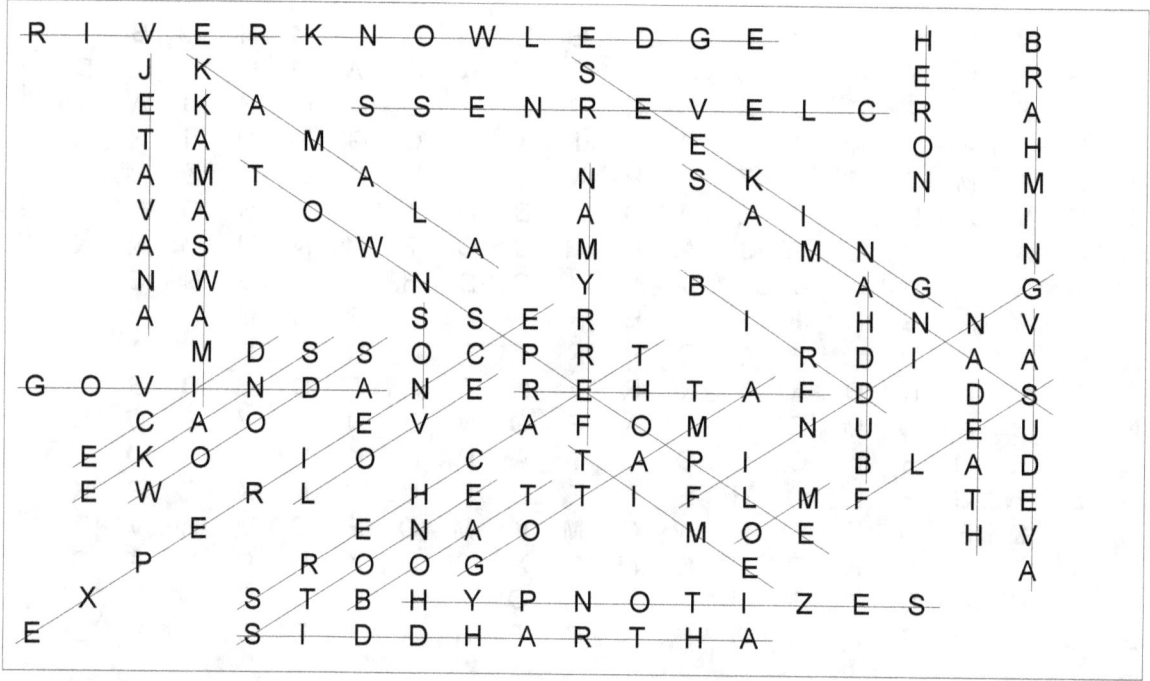

Buddha warns Siddhartha about too much of this. (10)
Businessman who befriended Siddhartha (9)
Courtesan who loved Siddhartha (6)
Faithful friend of Siddhartha since childhood (7)
He is recognized by his complete peacefulness. (6)
He steals a boat and runs away. (3)
He taught Siddhartha about the river. (8)
It means being receptive without a goal. (7)
It means having a goal. (7)
It symbolizes the flow of life. (5)
It symbolizes the transformation of Siddhartha. (5)
One of the two animals Siddhartha associates himself with (5)
Secret from the river: there is no such thing as ___. (4)
Siddhartha and Govinda joined them. (7)
Siddhartha became obsessed with this game. (4)
Siddhartha believes he must gain this for himself. (10)
Siddhartha desires to lose this. (4)

Siddhartha does this to the eldest Samana. (10)
Siddhartha dreamed that it died and he threw it away. (4)
Siddhartha longs for it after leaving Kamala. (5)
Siddhartha lost the desire to have these. (8)
Siddhartha saw him in his river reflection. (6)
Siddhartha tells Govinda that it could one day become a man. (5)
Siddhartha's father is one. (7)
Siddhartha's journey was to acquire this. (9)
Siddhartha's son's means of escape (4)
Son of a Brahmin who left home to find enlightenment (10)
Taught Siddhartha about the river (8)
The Buddha (6)
The Buddha forbade his followers to bind themselves to this. (4)
The Buddha was given this place in which to live. (8)
They loved and admired Siddhartha. (11)
Where the Ferryman goes to die. (5)
Word-sound that brings Siddhartha a sense of peace (2)

Siddhartha Word Search 2

```
F I N D I N G N I K E E S S K D E A T H
P A F S N T J K D M N N F A N I M H R B
S Q T D C Y Z E I O A P M M O C L D I T
J W J H L B V T T K Q A T A W E K D V Q
B Z Q E E V B S E A L D B N L H H U E Q
C I V K V R C R Z A V V Z A E P E B R Y
V O R Q E B H E R D J A Q S D P Q R J Y
L C D D R D E H H Q H S N Q G A B W O C
K K E C N Q L C Y V Y U P A E H C R N N
X L X X E L P A T K P D S K R T Q F K V
S V P V S X O E V D N E V J F R D G H B
L G E G S M E T Y M O V L G E A Z O Q S
L Q R G C L P C D T T A S Z R H D V G W
R M I G Q P S Q Q S I K Q F R D K I O Z
X V E H S Y N G D D Z T L N Y D N N T T
P C N H L X W O L N E E H X M I S D A Z
H C C G T A O B O N S K A M A S W A M I
F P E C G W T S B R A H M I N R L O A K
```

Buddha warns Siddhartha about too much of this. (10)
Businessman who befriended Siddhartha (9)
Courtesan who loved Siddhartha (6)
Faithful friend of Siddhartha since childhood (7)
He is recognized by his complete peacefulness. (6)
He steals a boat and runs away. (3)
He taught Siddhartha about the river. (8)
It means being receptive without a goal. (7)
It means having a goal. (7)
It symbolizes the flow of life. (5)
It symbolizes the transformation of Siddhartha. (5)
One of the two animals Siddhartha associates himself with (5)
Secret from the river: there is no such thing as ___. (4)
Siddhartha and Govinda joined them. (7)
Siddhartha became obsessed with this game. (4)
Siddhartha believes he must gain this for himself. (10)
Siddhartha desires to lose this. (4)

Siddhartha does this to the eldest Samana. (10)
Siddhartha dreamed that it died and he threw it away. (4)
Siddhartha longs for it after leaving Kamala. (5)
Siddhartha lost the desire to have these. (8)
Siddhartha saw him in his river reflection. (6)
Siddhartha tells Govinda that it could one day become a man. (5)
Siddhartha's father is one. (7)
Siddhartha's journey was to acquire this. (9)
Siddhartha's son's means of escape (4)
Son of a Brahmin who left home to find enlightenment (10)
Taught Siddhartha about the river (8)
The Buddha (6)
The Buddha forbade his followers to bind themselves to this. (4)
The Buddha was given this place in which to live. (8)
They loved and admired Siddhartha. (11)
Where the Ferryman goes to die. (5)
Word-sound that brings Siddhartha a sense of peace (2)

Siddhartha Word Search 2 Answer Key

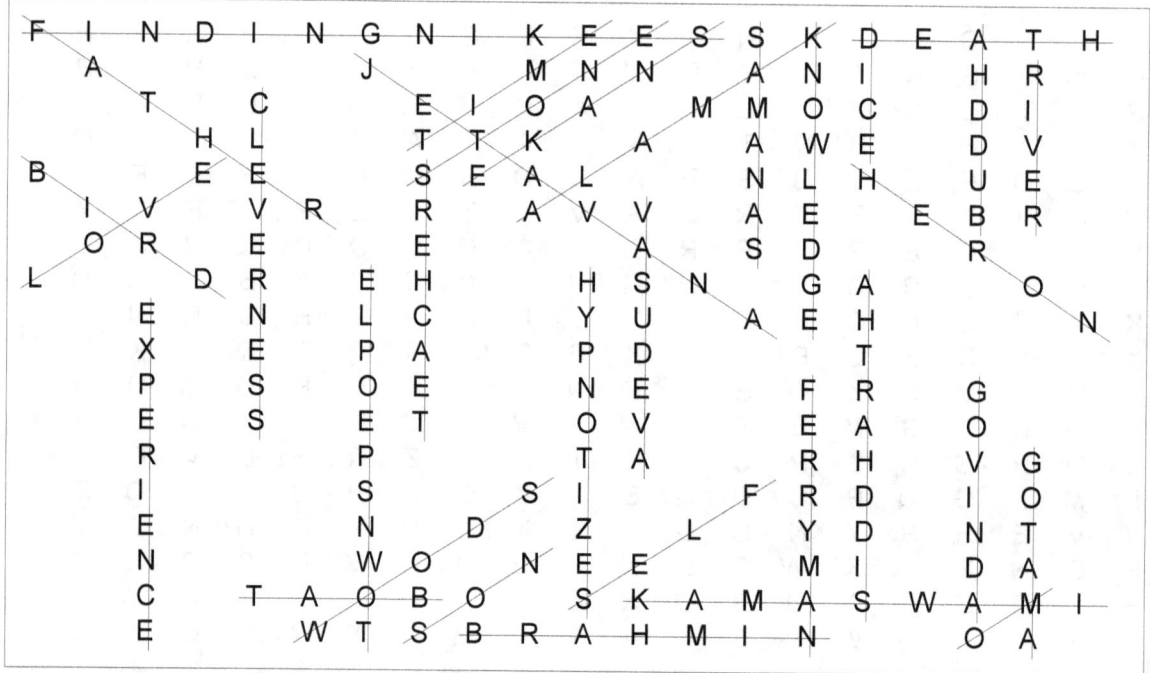

Buddha warns Siddhartha about too much of this. (10)
Businessman who befriended Siddhartha (9)
Courtesan who loved Siddhartha (6)
Faithful friend of Siddhartha since childhood (7)
He is recognized by his complete peacefulness. (6)
He steals a boat and runs away. (3)
He taught Siddhartha about the river. (8)
It means being receptive without a goal. (7)
It means having a goal. (7)
It symbolizes the flow of life. (5)
It symbolizes the transformation of Siddhartha. (5)
One of the two animals Siddhartha associates himself with (5)
Secret from the river: there is no such thing as ___. (4)
Siddhartha and Govinda joined them. (7)
Siddhartha became obsessed with this game. (4)
Siddhartha believes he must gain this for himself. (10)
Siddhartha desires to lose this. (4)

Siddhartha does this to the eldest Samana. (10)
Siddhartha dreamed that it died and he threw it away. (4)
Siddhartha longs for it after leaving Kamala. (5)
Siddhartha lost the desire to have these. (8)
Siddhartha saw him in his river reflection. (6)
Siddhartha tells Govinda that it could one day become a man. (5)
Siddhartha's father is one. (7)
Siddhartha's journey was to acquire this. (9)
Siddhartha's son's means of escape (4)
Son of a Brahmin who left home to find enlightenment (10)
Taught Siddhartha about the river (8)
The Buddha (6)
The Buddha forbade his followers to bind themselves to this. (4)
The Buddha was given this place in which to live. (8)
They loved and admired Siddhartha. (11)
Where the Ferryman goes to die. (5)
Word-sound that brings Siddhartha a sense of peace (2)

Siddhartha Word Search 3

```
S I D D H A R T H A Q T A J Q S V G B W
F Y W C X S R G O M P N X D X A L Z R N
F P X L H D H O W A C S R Z M M K A L M
D Q T E Y G J Z H V N B V V J A C N H M
B E N V P K S V A J I S F P X N F O M D
T X B E N N E T G R B N P K J A S W I G
M P U R O M E P O E P G D E H S D L N M
G E D N T J K X T H Z Y X A O D N E L H
S R D E I W I Z A T J K D X M P F D N M
H I H S Z N N K M A Y Z A Q Z L L G Y H
E E A S E G G N A F K N A M Y R R E F V
R N N Q S W C V L M I L F R A Y S M W Q
O C W B X H E E W R A N L X M L N I R P
N E E C I D S S O N W S D O B O A T I K
F Z R F U C W W O P L R W I V B K M V M
Z Q D S F B J T D H I M X A N E E K E F
D E A T H D B H S B Z D V F M G X C R S
F V S T O N E T E A C H E R S I G B D P
```

BIRD	GOVINDA	SELF
BOAT	HERON	SIDDHARTHA
BRAHMIN	HYPNOTIZES	SNAKE
BUDDHA	JETAVANA	SON
CLEVERNESS	KAMALA	STONE
DEATH	KAMASWAMI	TEACHERS
DICE	KNOWLEDGE	TIME
EXPERIENCE	LOVE	TOWNSPEOPLE
FATHER	OM	VASUDEVA
FERRYMAN	RIVER	WOODS
FINDING	SAMANAS	
GOTAMA	SEEKING	

Siddhartha Word Search 3 Answer Key

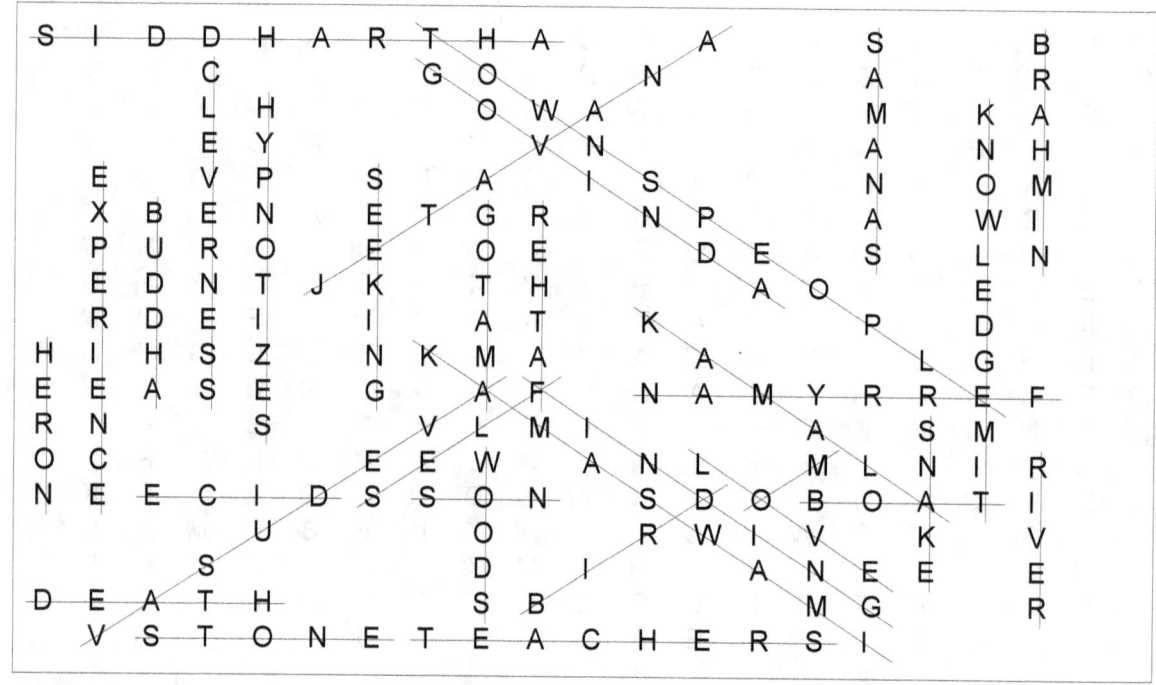

BIRD	GOVINDA	SELF
BOAT	HERON	SIDDHARTHA
BRAHMIN	HYPNOTIZES	SNAKE
BUDDHA	JETAVANA	SON
CLEVERNESS	KAMALA	STONE
DEATH	KAMASWAMI	TEACHERS
DICE	KNOWLEDGE	TIME
EXPERIENCE	LOVE	TOWNSPEOPLE
FATHER	OM	VASUDEVA
FERRYMAN	RIVER	WOODS
FINDING	SAMANAS	
GOTAMA	SEEKING	

Siddhartha Word Search 4

```
H F G D T I M E R T O W N S P E O P L E
Y Z F B W E V F F P G O V I N D A B F N
P G P X H O A S A Z Q O P H B S L O L Z
N Z F R L K J C T H X D J L J E B A E S
O G R Y G T H F H W K S T O N E Z T S D
T M C J O T D E E E N X C L C K F S W S
I F H K T Q K W R A R Y W I F I E K M S
Z I Z P A N D N K O G S D N X N N A A Y
E N R P M E V E O V N K O R R G R M D S
S D S J A Z X B S W T S E E T Z A A R L
R I C T S B D P K Z L V V G V N T S S S
H N H V R R R C E L I E S V A R J W T D
P G B I R D A A W R L K D S K A M A L A
Y P V S D H B H H C I J V G L L H M K W
Z N Y Y D C B P L M N E Q Z E G G I P P
Q M Q D T R C V B C I A N A V A T E J D
D R U F E R R Y M A N N H C Y Q Z D J H
Y B S I D D H A R T H A A V E D U S A V
```

BIRD

BOAT

BRAHMIN

BUDDHA

CLEVERNESS

DEATH

DICE

EXPERIENCE

FATHER

FERRYMAN

FINDING

GOTAMA

GOVINDA

HERON

HYPNOTIZES

JETAVANA

KAMALA

KAMASWAMI

KNOWLEDGE

LOVE

OM

RIVER

SAMANAS

SEEKING

SELF

SIDDHARTHA

SNAKE

SON

STONE

TEACHERS

TIME

TOWNSPEOPLE

VASUDEVA

WOODS

Siddhartha Word Search 4 Answer Key

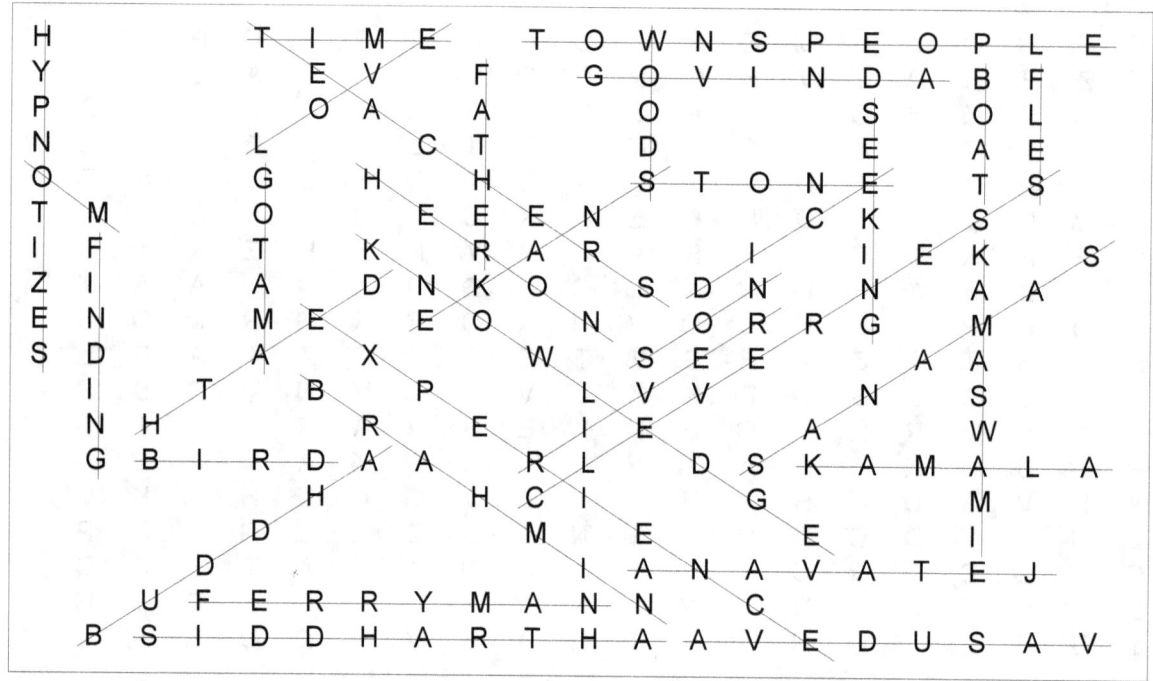

BIRD	GOVINDA	SELF
BOAT	HERON	SIDDHARTHA
BRAHMIN	HYPNOTIZES	SNAKE
BUDDHA	JETAVANA	SON
CLEVERNESS	KAMALA	STONE
DEATH	KAMASWAMI	TEACHERS
DICE	KNOWLEDGE	TIME
EXPERIENCE	LOVE	TOWNSPEOPLE
FATHER	OM	VASUDEVA
FERRYMAN	RIVER	WOODS
FINDING	SAMANAS	
GOTAMA	SEEKING	

Siddhartha Crossword 1

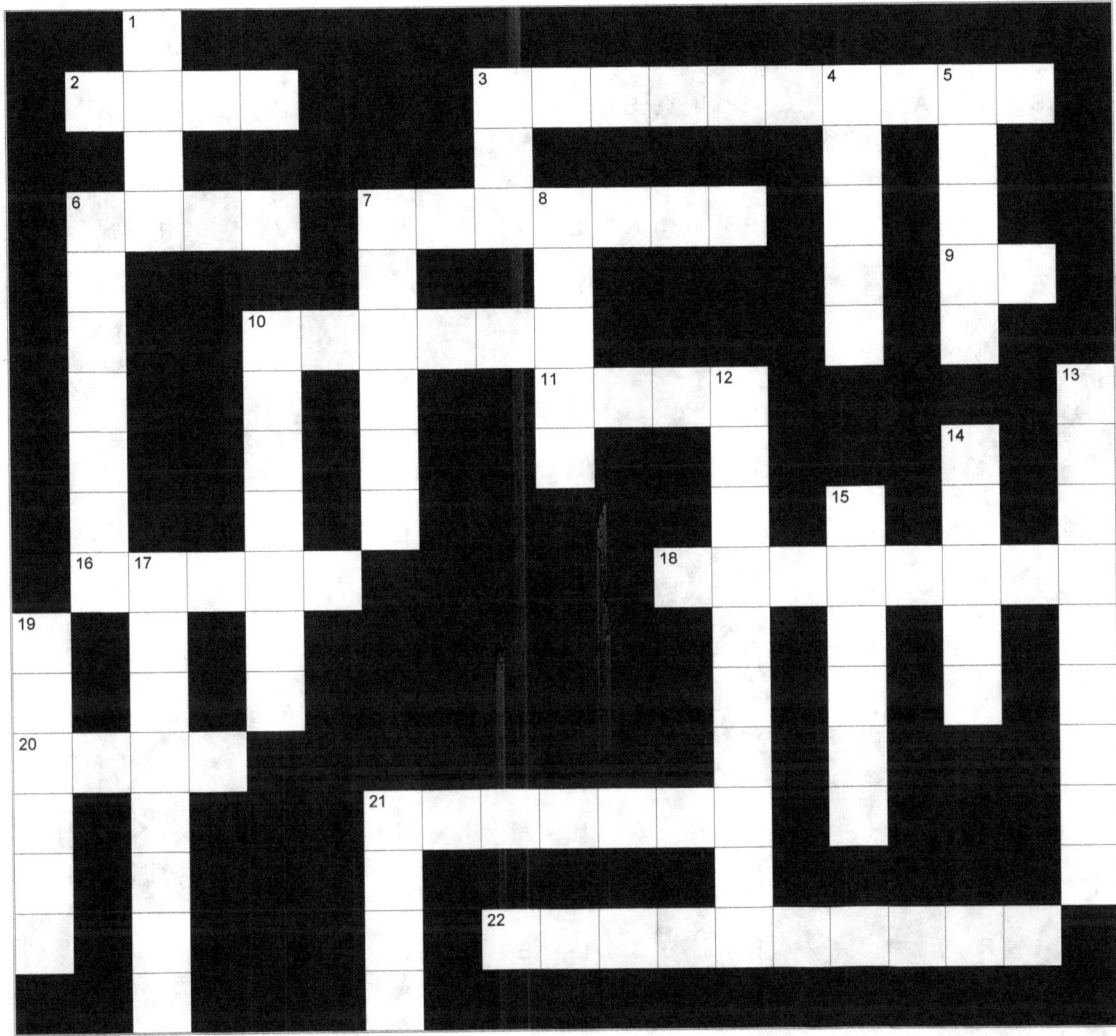

Across
2. Siddhartha's son's means of escape
3. Son of a Brahmin who left home to find enlightenment
6. Siddhartha desires to lose this.
7. It means being receptive without a goal.
9. Word-sound that brings Siddhartha a sense of peace
10. The Buddha
11. Secret from the river: there is no such thing as ___.
16. Siddhartha tells Govinda that it could one day become a man.
18. The Buddha was given this place in which to live.
20. Siddhartha became obsessed with this game.
21. Siddhartha's father is one.
22. Buddha warns Siddhartha about too much of this.

Down
1. The Buddha forbade his followers to bind themselves to this.
3. He steals a boat and runs away.
4. It symbolizes the flow of life.
5. One of the two animals Siddhartha associates himself with
6. Siddhartha and Govinda joined them.
7. Siddhartha saw him in his river reflection.
8. Siddhartha longs for it after leaving Kamala.
10. Faithful friend of Siddhartha since childhood
12. Siddhartha believes he must gain this for himself.
13. Businessman who befriended Siddhartha
14. It symbolizes the transformation of Siddhartha.
15. Courtesan who loved Siddhartha
17. Siddhartha lost the desire to have these.
19. He is recognized by his complete peacefulness.
21. Siddhartha dreamed that it died and he threw it away.

Siddhartha Crossword 1 Answer Key

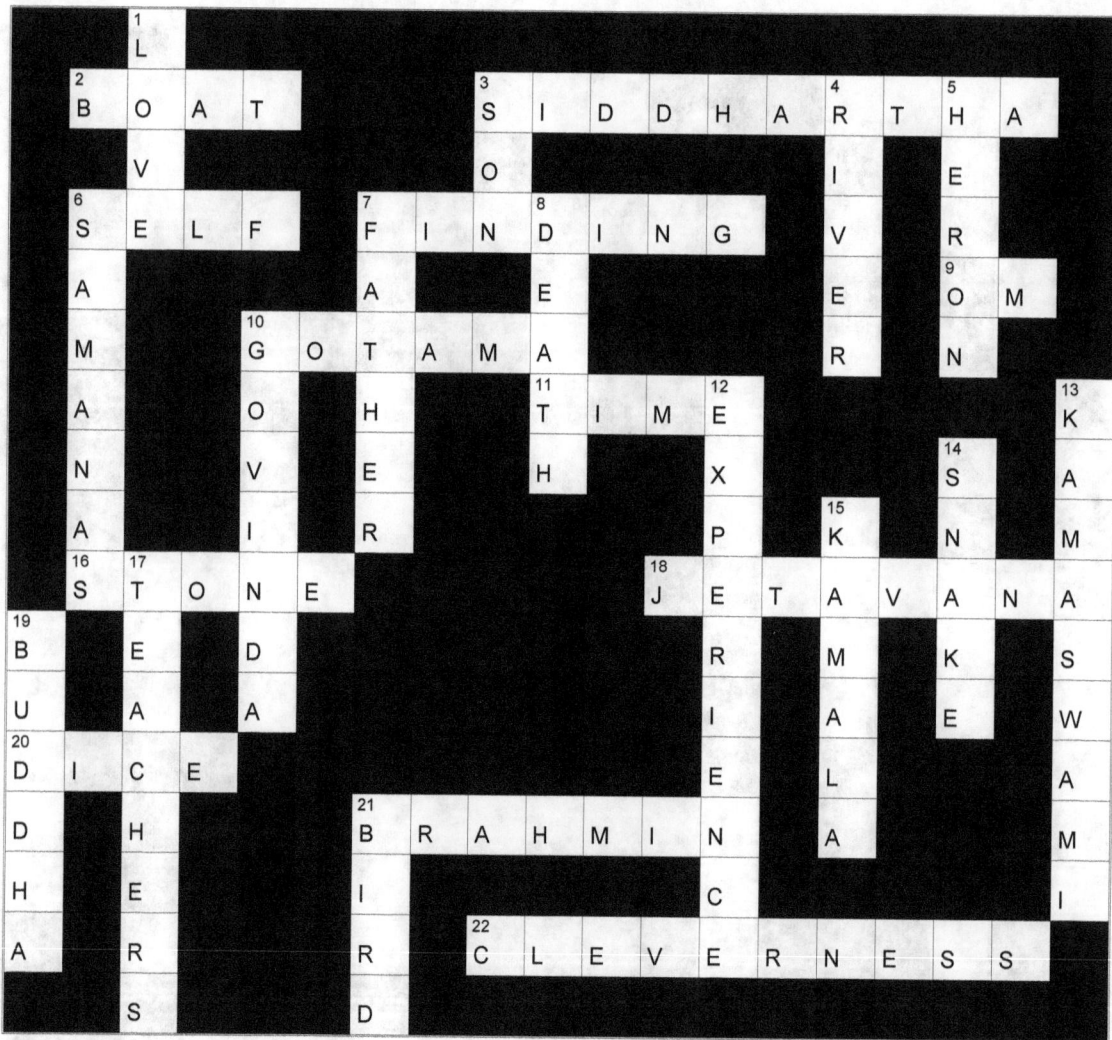

Across
2. Siddhartha's son's means of escape
3. Son of a Brahmin who left home to find enlightenment
6. Siddhartha desires to lose this.
7. It means being receptive without a goal.
9. Word-sound that brings Siddhartha a sense of peace
10. The Buddha
11. Secret from the river: there is no such thing as ___.
16. Siddhartha tells Govinda that it could one day become a man.
18. The Buddha was given this place in which to live.
20. Siddhartha became obsessed with this game.
21. Siddhartha's father is one.
22. Buddha warns Siddhartha about too much of this.

Down
1. The Buddha forbade his followers to bind themselves to this.
3. He steals a boat and runs away.
4. It symbolizes the flow of life.
5. One of the two animals Siddhartha associates himself with
6. Siddhartha and Govinda joined them.
7. Siddhartha saw him in his river reflection.
8. Siddhartha longs for it after leaving Kamala.
10. Faithful friend of Siddhartha since childhood
12. Siddhartha believes he must gain this for himself.
13. Businessman who befriended Siddhartha
14. It symbolizes the transformation of Siddhartha.
15. Courtesan who loved Siddhartha
17. Siddhartha lost the desire to have these.
19. He is recognized by his complete peacefulness.
21. Siddhartha dreamed that it died and he threw it away.

Siddhartha Crossword 2

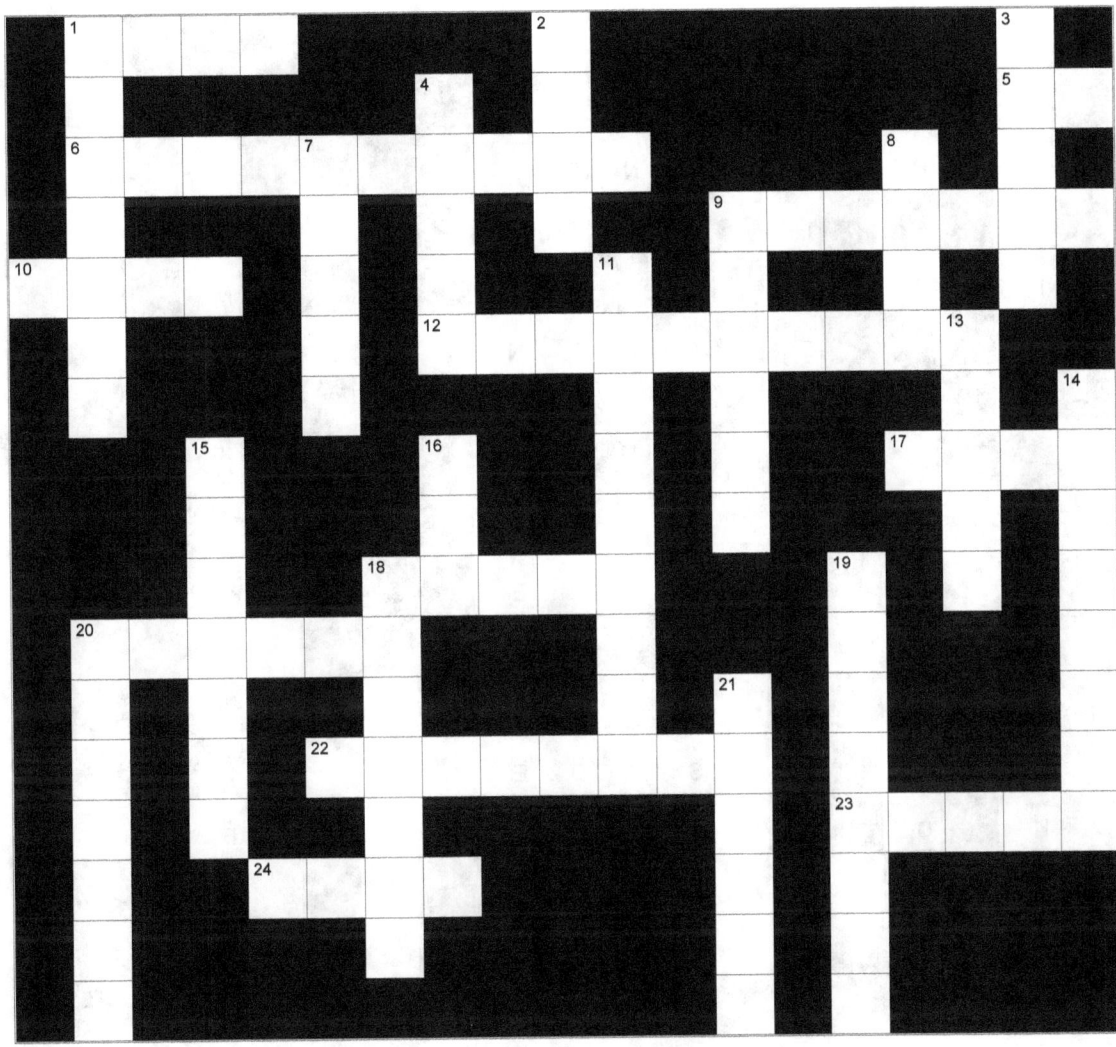

Across
1. Siddhartha desires to lose this.
5. Word-sound that brings Siddhartha a sense of peace
6. Siddhartha believes he must gain this for himself.
9. Faithful friend of Siddhartha since childhood
10. Siddhartha dreamed that it died and he threw it away.
12. Siddhartha does this to the eldest Samana.
17. The Buddha forbade his followers to bind themselves to this.
18. It symbolizes the transformation of Siddhartha.
20. He is recognized by his complete peacefulness.
22. He taught Siddhartha about the river.
23. One of the two animals Siddhartha associates himself with
24. Siddhartha's son's means of escape

Down
1. It means having a goal.
2. Siddhartha became obsessed with this game.
3. Where the Ferryman goes to die.
4. Siddhartha longs for it after leaving Kamala.
7. It symbolizes the flow of life.
8. Secret from the river: there is no such thing as ___.
9. The Buddha
11. Siddhartha's journey was to acquire this.
13. Siddhartha tells Govinda that it could one day become a man.
14. Taught Siddhartha about the river
15. It means being receptive without a goal.
16. He steals a boat and runs away.
18. Siddhartha and Govinda joined them.
19. Siddhartha lost the desire to have these.
20. Siddhartha's father is one.
21. Siddhartha saw him in his river reflection.

Siddhartha Crossword 2 Answer Key

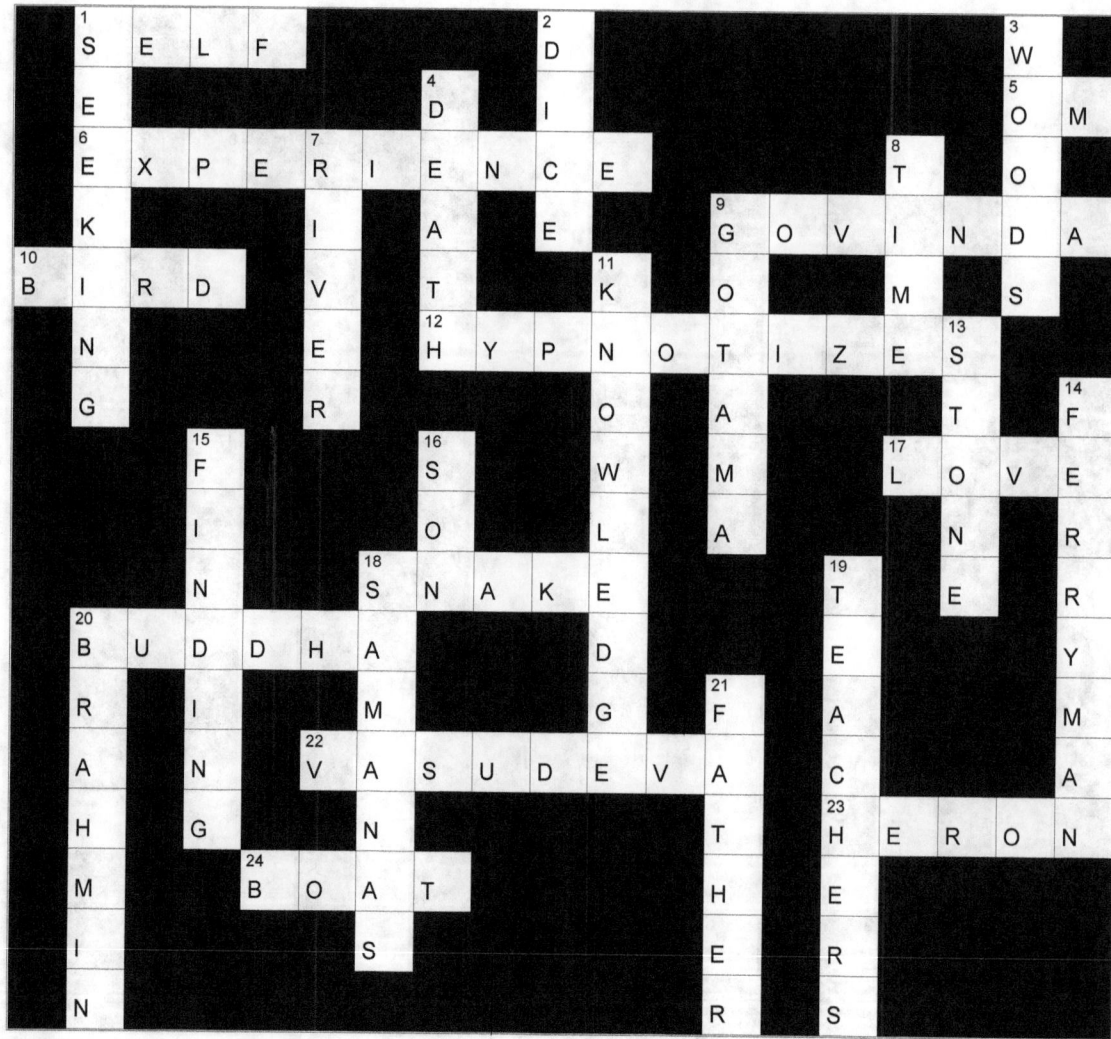

Across
1. Siddhartha desires to lose this.
5. Word-sound that brings Siddhartha a sense of peace
6. Siddhartha believes he must gain this for himself.
9. Faithful friend of Siddhartha since childhood
10. Siddhartha dreamed that it died and he threw it away.
12. Siddhartha does this to the eldest Samana.
17. The Buddha forbade his followers to bind themselves to this.
18. It symbolizes the transformation of Siddhartha.
20. He is recognized by his complete peacefulness.
22. He taught Siddhartha about the river.
23. One of the two animals Siddhartha associates himself with
24. Siddhartha's son's means of escape

Down
1. It means having a goal.
2. Siddhartha became obsessed with this game.
3. Where the Ferryman goes to die.
4. Siddhartha longs for it after leaving Kamala.
7. It symbolizes the flow of life.
8. Secret from the river: there is no such thing as ___.
9. The Buddha
11. Siddhartha's journey was to acquire this.
13. Siddhartha tells Govinda that it could one day become a man.
14. Taught Siddhartha about the river
15. It means being receptive without a goal.
16. He steals a boat and runs away.
18. Siddhartha and Govinda joined them.
19. Siddhartha lost the desire to have these.
20. Siddhartha's father is one.
21. Siddhartha saw him in his river reflection.

Siddhartha Crossword 3

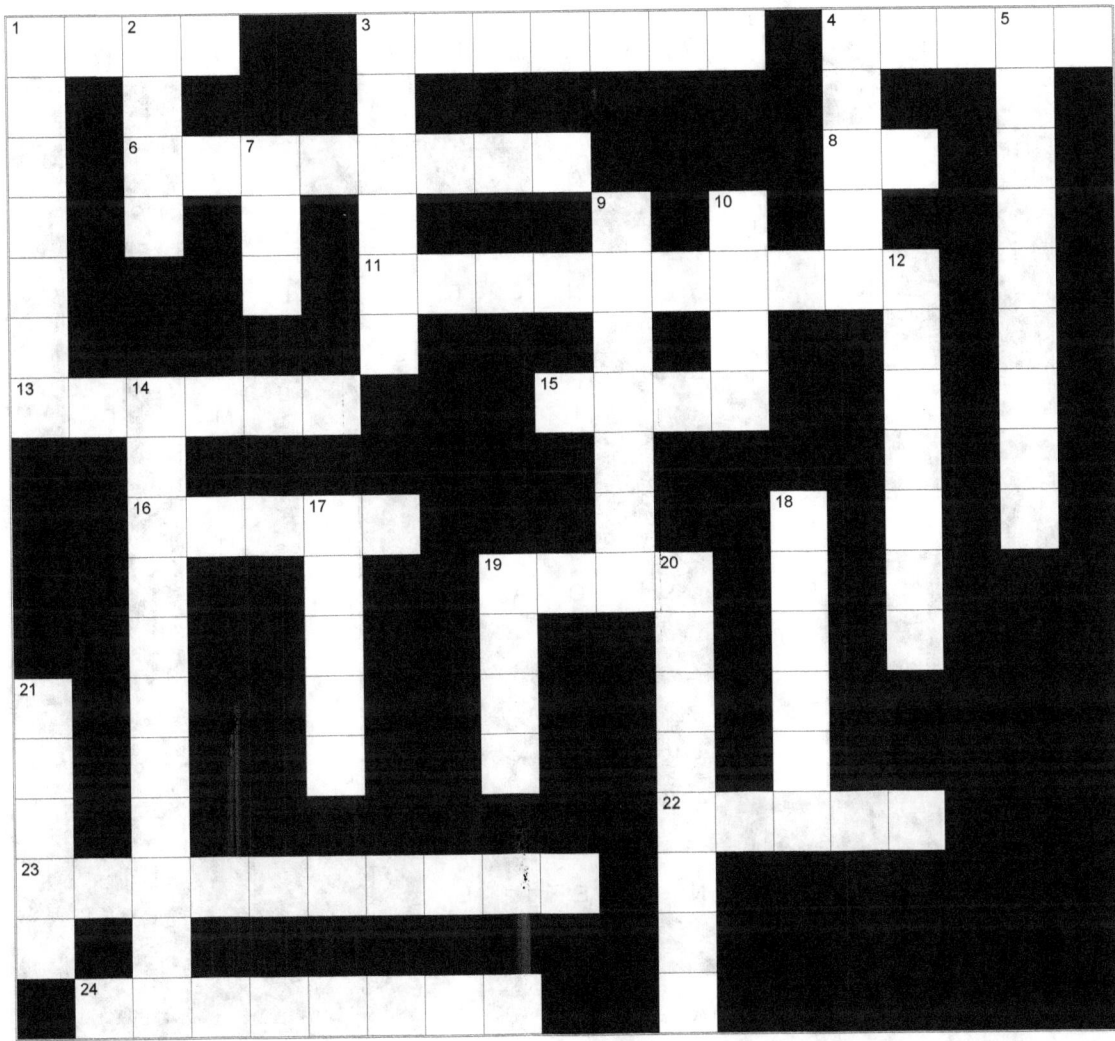

Across
1. Siddhartha desires to lose this.
3. Siddhartha's father is one.
4. It symbolizes the transformation of Siddhartha.
6. He taught Siddhartha about the river.
8. Word-sound that brings Siddhartha a sense of peace
11. Siddhartha does this to the eldest Samana.
13. The Buddha
15. Secret from the river: there is no such thing as ____.
16. Where the Ferryman goes to die.
19. Siddhartha's son's means of escape
22. One of the two animals Siddhartha associates himself with
23. Siddhartha believes he must gain this for himself.
24. Taught Siddhartha about the river

Down
1. It means having a goal.
2. The Buddha forbade his followers to bind themselves to this.
3. He is recognized by his complete peacefulness.
4. Siddhartha tells Govinda that it could one day become a man.
5. Siddhartha's journey was to acquire this.
7. He steals a boat and runs away.
9. Faithful friend of Siddhartha since childhood
10. Siddhartha became obsessed with this game.
12. Siddhartha and Govinda joined them.
14. They loved and admired Siddhartha.
17. Siddhartha longs for it after leaving Kamala.
18. Siddhartha saw him in his river reflection.
19. Siddhartha dreamed that it died and he threw it away.
20. Siddhartha lost the desire to have these.
21. It symbolizes the flow of life.

Siddhartha Crossword 3 Answer Key

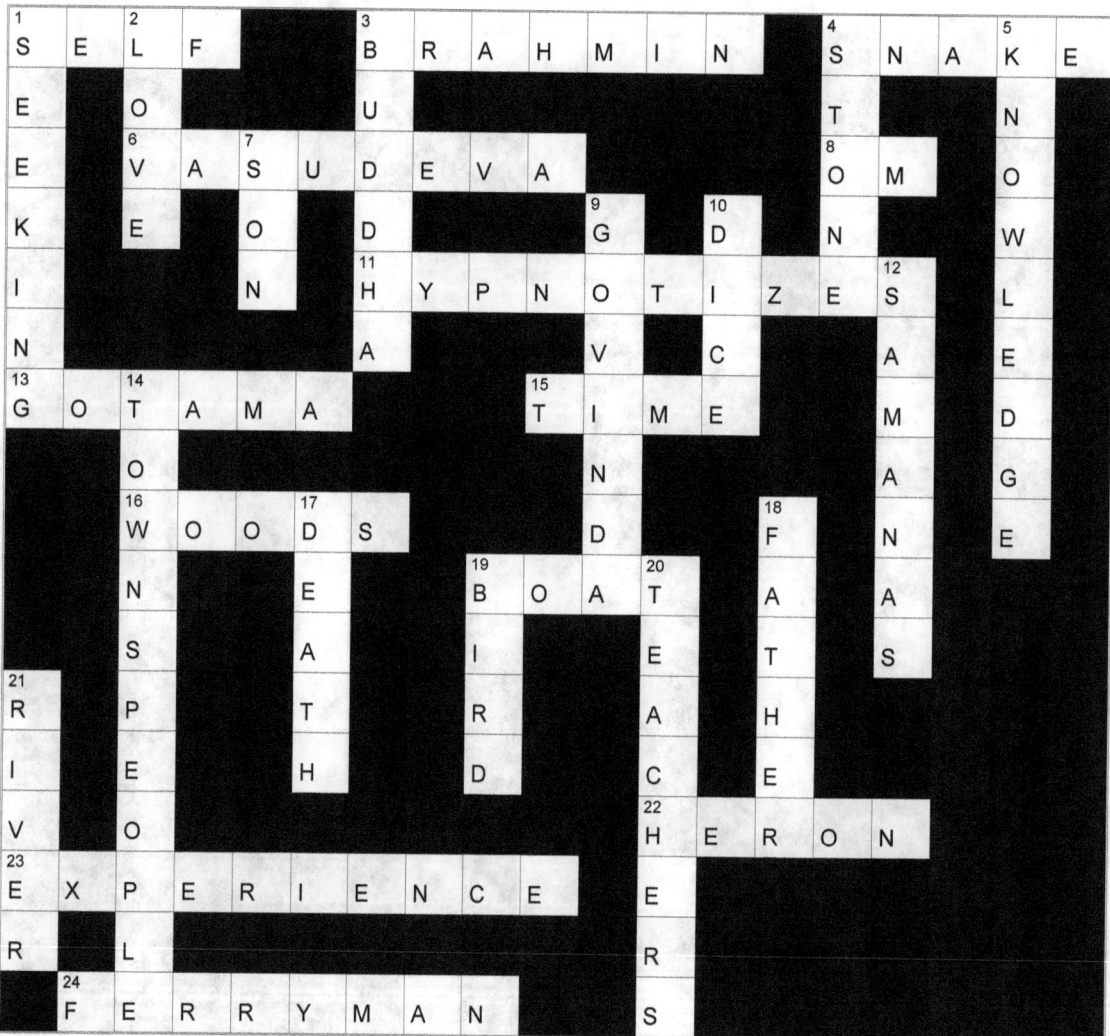

Across
1. Siddhartha desires to lose this.
3. Siddhartha's father is one.
4. It symbolizes the transformation of Siddhartha.
6. He taught Siddhartha about the river.
8. Word-sound that brings Siddhartha a sense of peace
11. Siddhartha does this to the eldest Samana.
13. The Buddha
15. Secret from the river: there is no such thing as ___.
16. Where the Ferryman goes to die.
19. Siddhartha's son's means of escape
22. One of the two animals Siddhartha associates himself with
23. Siddhartha believes he must gain this for himself.
24. Taught Siddhartha about the river

Down
1. It means having a goal.
2. The Buddha forbade his followers to bind themselves to this.
3. He is recognized by his complete peacefulness.
4. Siddhartha tells Govinda that it could one day become a man.
5. Siddhartha's journey was to acquire this.
7. He steals a boat and runs away.
9. Faithful friend of Siddhartha since childhood
10. Siddhartha became obsessed with this game.
12. Siddhartha and Govinda joined them.
14. They loved and admired Siddhartha.
17. Siddhartha longs for it after leaving Kamala.
18. Siddhartha saw him in his river reflection.
19. Siddhartha dreamed that it died and he threw it away.
20. Siddhartha lost the desire to have these.
21. It symbolizes the flow of life.

Siddhartha Crossword 4

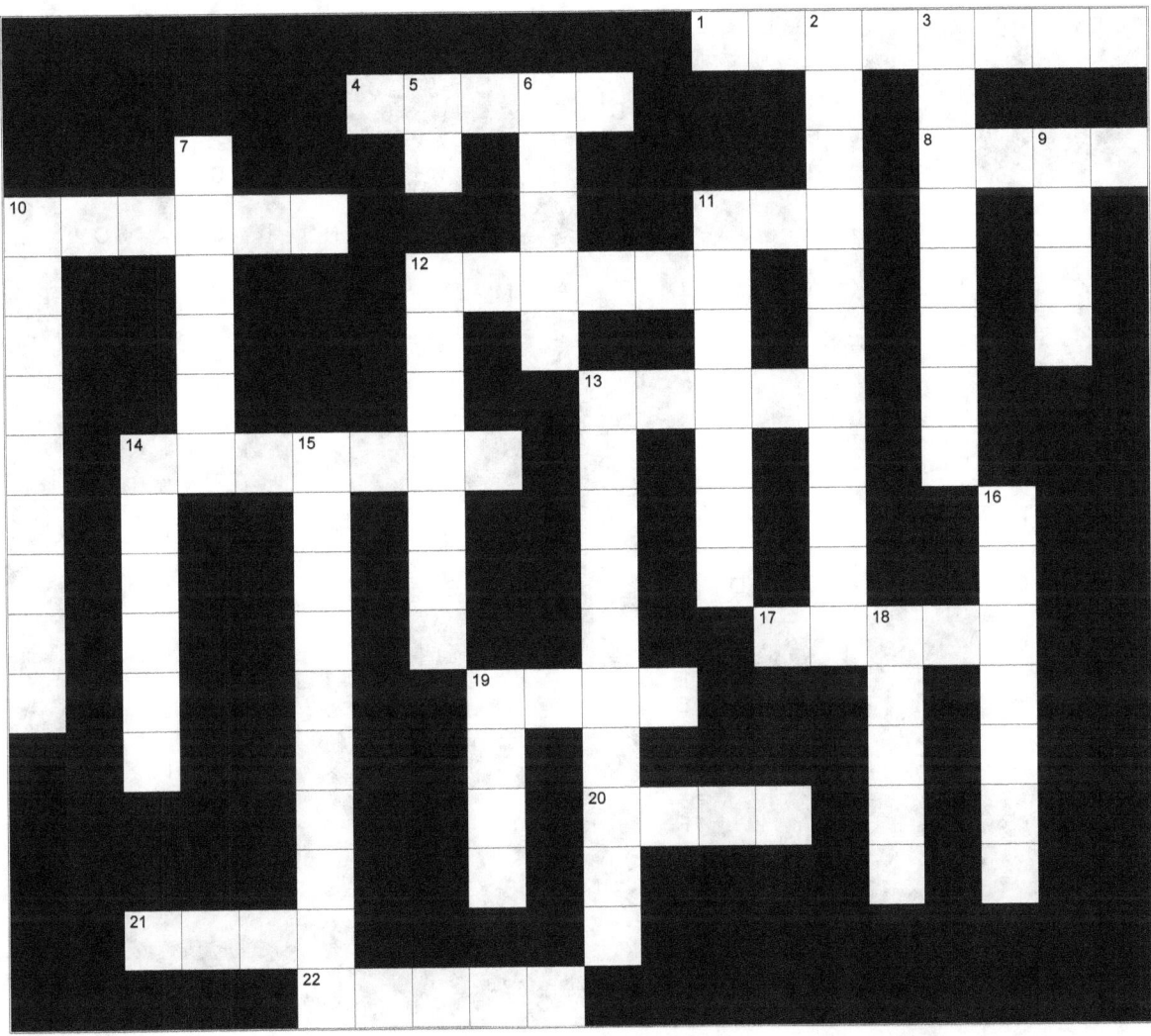

Across
1. The Buddha was given this place in which to live.
4. Where the Ferryman goes to die.
8. Siddhartha desires to lose this.
10. Courtesan who loved Siddhartha
11. He steals a boat and runs away.
12. The Buddha
13. It symbolizes the transformation of Siddhartha.
14. Siddhartha's father is one.
17. One of the two animals Siddhartha associates himself with
19. Siddhartha's son's means of escape
20. Secret from the river: there is no such thing as ___.
21. Siddhartha became obsessed with this game.
22. Siddhartha tells Govinda that it could one day become a man.

Down
2. They loved and admired Siddhartha.
3. He taught Siddhartha about the river.
5. Word-sound that brings Siddhartha a sense of peace
6. Siddhartha longs for it after leaving Kamala.
7. Siddhartha saw him in his river reflection.
9. The Buddha forbade his followers to bind themselves to this.
10. Siddhartha's journey was to acquire this.
11. Siddhartha and Govinda joined them.
12. Faithful friend of Siddhartha since childhood
13. Son of a Brahmin who left home to find enlightenment
14. He is recognized by his complete peacefulness.
15. Siddhartha does this to the eldest Samana.
16. It means being receptive without a goal.
18. It symbolizes the flow of life.
19. Siddhartha dreamed that it died and he threw it away.

Siddhartha Crossword 4 Answer Key

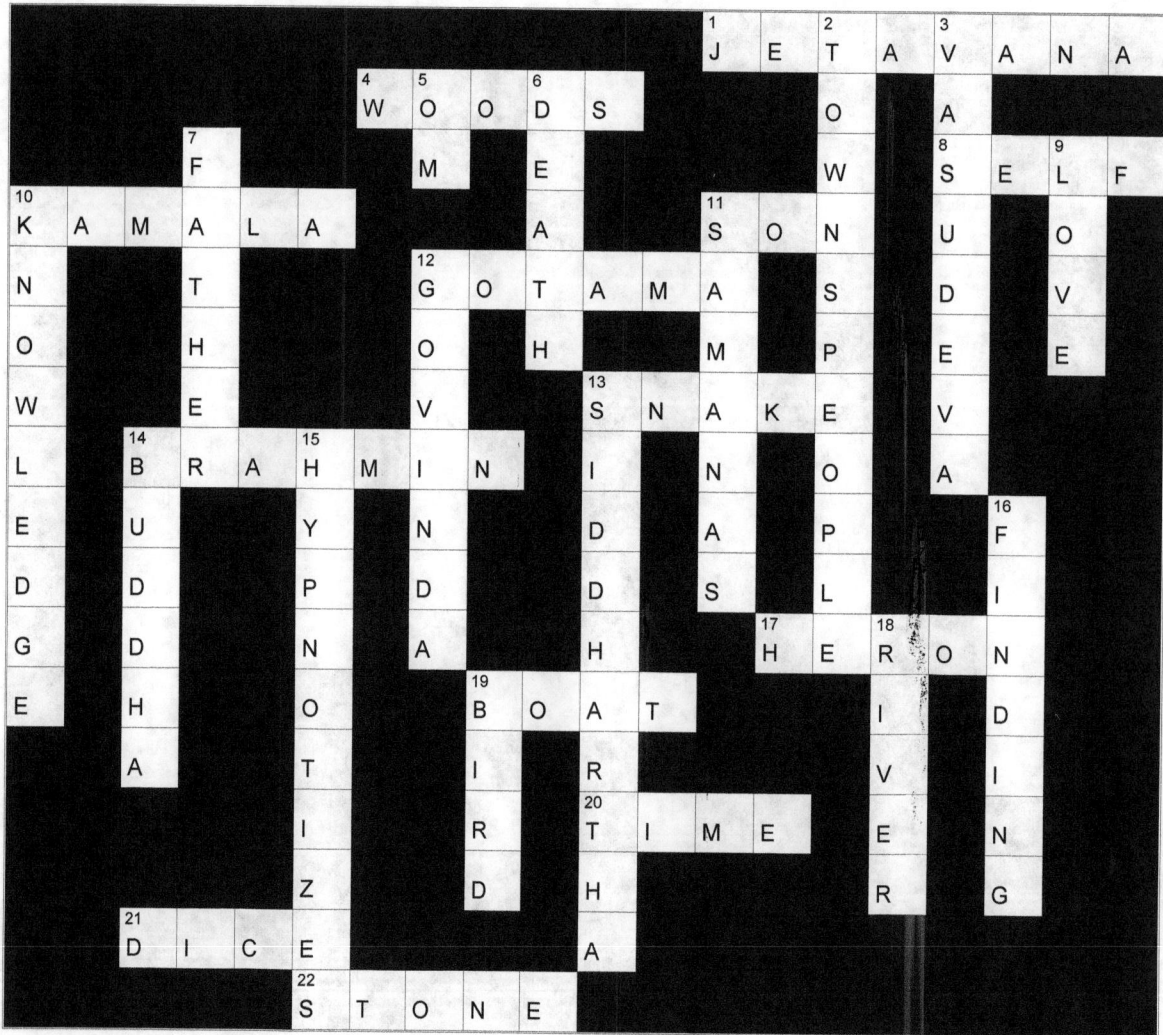

Across

1. The Buddha was given this place in which to live.
4. Where the Ferryman goes to die.
8. Siddhartha desires to lose this.
10. Courtesan who loved Siddhartha
11. He steals a boat and runs away.
12. The Buddha
13. It symbolizes the transformation of Siddhartha.
14. Siddhartha's father is one.
17. One of the two animals Siddhartha associates himself with
19. Siddhartha's son's means of escape
20. Secret from the river: there is no such thing as ___.
21. Siddhartha became obsessed with this game.
22. Siddhartha tells Govinda that it could one day become a man.

Down

2. They loved and admired Siddhartha.
3. He taught Siddhartha about the river.
5. Word-sound that brings Siddhartha a sense of peace
6. Siddhartha longs for it after leaving Kamala.
7. Siddhartha saw him in his river reflection.
9. The Buddha forbade his followers to bind themselves to this.
10. Siddhartha's journey was to acquire this.
11. Siddhartha and Govinda joined them.
12. Faithful friend of Siddhartha since childhood
13. Son of a Brahmin who left home to find enlightenment
14. He is recognized by his complete peacefulness.
15. Siddhartha does this to the eldest Samana.
16. It means being receptive without a goal.
18. It symbolizes the flow of life.
19. Siddhartha dreamed that it died and he threw it away.

Siddhartha

FATHER	BRAHMIN	DICE	TOWNSPEOPLE	HYPNOTIZES
KNOWLEDGE	RIVER	BOAT	SELF	SON
BUDDHA	KAMALA	FREE SPACE	KAMASWAMI	FERRYMAN
SEEKING	CLEVERNESS	SIDDHARTHA	SAMANAS	DEATH
TEACHERS	SNAKE	JETAVANA	LOVE	WOODS

Siddhartha

TIME	EXPERIENCE	VASUDEVA	GOVINDA	HERON
GOTAMA	STONE	BIRD	OM	WOODS
LOVE	JETAVANA	FREE SPACE	TEACHERS	DEATH
SAMANAS	SIDDHARTHA	CLEVERNESS	SEEKING	FERRYMAN
KAMASWAMI	FINDING	KAMALA	BUDDHA	SON

Siddhartha

HYPNOTIZES	KAMASWAMI	BRAHMIN	SNAKE	DICE
SELF	STONE	GOVINDA	DEATH	SON
JETAVANA	TIME	FREE SPACE	WOODS	TOWNSPEOPLE
BUDDHA	GOTAMA	LOVE	KAMALA	EXPERIENCE
HERON	VASUDEVA	SEEKING	CLEVERNESS	FATHER

Siddhartha

TEACHERS	OM	KNOWLEDGE	SAMANAS	SIDDHARTHA
RIVER	BIRD	BOAT	FINDING	FATHER
CLEVERNESS	SEEKING	FREE SPACE	HERON	EXPERIENCE
KAMALA	LOVE	GOTAMA	BUDDHA	TOWNSPEOPLE
WOODS	FERRYMAN	TIME	JETAVANA	SON

Siddhartha

TIME	EXPERIENCE	LOVE	SELF	DICE
TOWNSPEOPLE	HERON	VASUDEVA	FINDING	CLEVERNESS
KNOWLEDGE	GOVINDA	FREE SPACE	RIVER	BRAHMIN
SIDDHARTHA	STONE	TEACHERS	SEEKING	JETAVANA
GOTAMA	WOODS	SAMANAS	KAMALA	FERRYMAN

Siddhartha

SNAKE	BUDDHA	SON	KAMASWAMI	BOAT
DEATH	FATHER	HYPNOTIZES	OM	FERRYMAN
KAMALA	SAMANAS	FREE SPACE	GOTAMA	JETAVANA
SEEKING	TEACHERS	STONE	SIDDHARTHA	BRAHMIN
RIVER	BIRD	GOVINDA	KNOWLEDGE	CLEVERNESS

Siddhartha

FATHER	JETAVANA	BIRD	FERRYMAN	HYPNOTIZES
SELF	KAMASWAMI	OM	GOVINDA	STONE
DEATH	BUDDHA	FREE SPACE	RIVER	BOAT
LOVE	HERON	SON	EXPERIENCE	KNOWLEDGE
SAMANAS	DICE	GOTAMA	TOWNSPEOPLE	TIME

Siddhartha

KAMALA	CLEVERNESS	VASUDEVA	WOODS	SNAKE
BRAHMIN	SIDDHARTHA	SEEKING	TEACHERS	TIME
TOWNSPEOPLE	GOTAMA	FREE SPACE	SAMANAS	KNOWLEDGE
EXPERIENCE	SON	HERON	LOVE	BOAT
RIVER	FINDING	BUDDHA	DEATH	STONE

Siddhartha

BOAT	BUDDHA	FINDING	TEACHERS	DEATH
LOVE	SELF	VASUDEVA	HERON	GOVINDA
SEEKING	KAMALA	FREE SPACE	SNAKE	EXPERIENCE
BIRD	GOTAMA	KNOWLEDGE	DICE	KAMASWAMI
SON	TIME	BRAHMIN	CLEVERNESS	OM

Siddhartha

FERRYMAN	STONE	RIVER	SAMANAS	JETAVANA
FATHER	WOODS	SIDDHARTHA	HYPNOTIZES	OM
CLEVERNESS	BRAHMIN	FREE SPACE	SON	KAMASWAMI
DICE	KNOWLEDGE	GOTAMA	BIRD	EXPERIENCE
SNAKE	TOWNSPEOPLE	KAMALA	SEEKING	GOVINDA

Siddhartha

CLEVERNESS	BIRD	SNAKE	VASUDEVA	BOAT
KNOWLEDGE	SAMANAS	EXPERIENCE	SELF	TIME
SON	DICE	FREE SPACE	FINDING	LOVE
HERON	BUDDHA	HYPNOTIZES	SEEKING	WOODS
TEACHERS	GOVINDA	TOWNSPEOPLE	RIVER	FERRYMAN

Siddhartha

DEATH	FATHER	OM	GOTAMA	STONE
KAMALA	BRAHMIN	SIDDHARTHA	JETAVANA	FERRYMAN
RIVER	TOWNSPEOPLE	FREE SPACE	TEACHERS	WOODS
SEEKING	HYPNOTIZES	BUDDHA	HERON	LOVE
FINDING	KAMASWAMI	DICE	SON	TIME

Siddhartha

KAMASWAMI	BOAT	BIRD	HYPNOTIZES	RIVER
DICE	TIME	KNOWLEDGE	HERON	TOWNSPEOPLE
CLEVERNESS	VASUDEVA	FREE SPACE	BRAHMIN	OM
SEEKING	DEATH	FINDING	TEACHERS	SELF
KAMALA	SON	JETAVANA	WOODS	LOVE

Siddhartha

FATHER	EXPERIENCE	STONE	SIDDHARTHA	SNAKE
BUDDHA	GOVINDA	FERRYMAN	SAMANAS	LOVE
WOODS	JETAVANA	FREE SPACE	KAMALA	SELF
TEACHERS	FINDING	DEATH	SEEKING	OM
BRAHMIN	GOTAMA	VASUDEVA	CLEVERNESS	TOWNSPEOPLE

Siddhartha

KAMALA	DICE	SAMANAS	BOAT	SELF
GOTAMA	BRAHMIN	EXPERIENCE	SIDDHARTHA	FATHER
KNOWLEDGE	DEATH	FREE SPACE	BIRD	CLEVERNESS
SEEKING	SNAKE	HERON	TOWNSPEOPLE	GOVINDA
TIME	LOVE	HYPNOTIZES	KAMASWAMI	FINDING

Siddhartha

WOODS	OM	SON	BUDDHA	TEACHERS
STONE	RIVER	VASUDEVA	JETAVANA	FINDING
KAMASWAMI	HYPNOTIZES	FREE SPACE	TIME	GOVINDA
TOWNSPEOPLE	HERON	SNAKE	SEEKING	CLEVERNESS
BIRD	FERRYMAN	DEATH	KNOWLEDGE	FATHER

Siddhartha

SELF	SAMANAS	SIDDHARTHA	BRAHMIN	FATHER
SNAKE	KNOWLEDGE	TIME	GOVINDA	JETAVANA
HERON	BUDDHA	FREE SPACE	KAMASWAMI	STONE
FERRYMAN	TEACHERS	RIVER	BIRD	FINDING
HYPNOTIZES	DEATH	WOODS	KAMALA	SEEKING

Siddhartha

CLEVERNESS	BOAT	VASUDEVA	DICE	TOWNSPEOPLE
EXPERIENCE	OM	LOVE	SON	SEEKING
KAMALA	WOODS	FREE SPACE	HYPNOTIZES	FINDING
BIRD	RIVER	TEACHERS	FERRYMAN	STONE
KAMASWAMI	GOTAMA	BUDDHA	HERON	JETAVANA

Siddhartha

SEEKING	HERON	CLEVERNESS	HYPNOTIZES	GOTAMA
BRAHMIN	TEACHERS	JETAVANA	LOVE	FATHER
SAMANAS	TOWNSPEOPLE	FREE SPACE	KAMALA	STONE
BIRD	KNOWLEDGE	EXPERIENCE	SNAKE	BOAT
BUDDHA	OM	DICE	FINDING	FERRYMAN

Siddhartha

KAMASWAMI	TIME	SON	GOVINDA	DEATH
VASUDEVA	SELF	SIDDHARTHA	WOODS	FERRYMAN
FINDING	DICE	FREE SPACE	BUDDHA	BOAT
SNAKE	EXPERIENCE	KNOWLEDGE	BIRD	STONE
KAMALA	RIVER	TOWNSPEOPLE	SAMANAS	FATHER

Siddhartha

CLEVERNESS	STONE	DEATH	SAMANAS	SON
JETAVANA	BRAHMIN	GOVINDA	BOAT	KAMASWAMI
HYPNOTIZES	EXPERIENCE	FREE SPACE	KAMALA	TEACHERS
VASUDEVA	SELF	SEEKING	FINDING	BUDDHA
FERRYMAN	HERON	KNOWLEDGE	FATHER	OM

Siddhartha

LOVE	TOWNSPEOPLE	WOODS	BIRD	SIDDHARTHA
SNAKE	TIME	GOTAMA	DICE	OM
FATHER	KNOWLEDGE	FREE SPACE	FERRYMAN	BUDDHA
FINDING	SEEKING	SELF	VASUDEVA	TEACHERS
KAMALA	RIVER	EXPERIENCE	HYPNOTIZES	KAMASWAMI

Siddhartha

SEEKING	DEATH	EXPERIENCE	FATHER	BOAT
DICE	JETAVANA	GOVINDA	LOVE	FINDING
CLEVERNESS	TEACHERS	FREE SPACE	KNOWLEDGE	TIME
TOWNSPEOPLE	SAMANAS	OM	BUDDHA	HYPNOTIZES
RIVER	KAMALA	GOTAMA	HERON	SELF

Siddhartha

STONE	SIDDHARTHA	BRAHMIN	BIRD	SON
SNAKE	VASUDEVA	WOODS	KAMASWAMI	SELF
HERON	GOTAMA	FREE SPACE	RIVER	HYPNOTIZES
BUDDHA	OM	SAMANAS	TOWNSPEOPLE	TIME
KNOWLEDGE	FERRYMAN	TEACHERS	CLEVERNESS	FINDING

Siddhartha

BRAHMIN	SAMANAS	DEATH	SEEKING	OM
BIRD	FINDING	HYPNOTIZES	FATHER	LOVE
SNAKE	VASUDEVA	FREE SPACE	EXPERIENCE	SON
TOWNSPEOPLE	RIVER	KAMALA	CLEVERNESS	SELF
BUDDHA	KAMASWAMI	JETAVANA	DICE	WOODS

Siddhartha

BOAT	SIDDHARTHA	STONE	KNOWLEDGE	TIME
GOTAMA	GOVINDA	FERRYMAN	HERON	WOODS
DICE	JETAVANA	FREE SPACE	BUDDHA	SELF
CLEVERNESS	KAMALA	RIVER	TOWNSPEOPLE	SON
EXPERIENCE	TEACHERS	VASUDEVA	SNAKE	LOVE

Siddhartha

DICE	BUDDHA	KNOWLEDGE	SNAKE	RIVER
STONE	HERON	CLEVERNESS	FATHER	SAMANAS
SIDDHARTHA	OM	FREE SPACE	KAMALA	WOODS
TEACHERS	JETAVANA	LOVE	KAMASWAMI	SELF
VASUDEVA	FINDING	EXPERIENCE	FERRYMAN	SEEKING

Siddhartha

GOVINDA	GOTAMA	BOAT	TOWNSPEOPLE	SON
TIME	DEATH	BIRD	BRAHMIN	SEEKING
FERRYMAN	EXPERIENCE	FREE SPACE	VASUDEVA	SELF
KAMASWAMI	LOVE	JETAVANA	TEACHERS	WOODS
KAMALA	HYPNOTIZES	OM	SIDDHARTHA	SAMANAS

Siddhartha

FINDING	KAMALA	DICE	BRAHMIN	LOVE
SNAKE	GOTAMA	VASUDEVA	WOODS	TOWNSPEOPLE
FATHER	HERON	FREE SPACE	KNOWLEDGE	JETAVANA
KAMASWAMI	SON	BIRD	EXPERIENCE	SIDDHARTHA
HYPNOTIZES	TEACHERS	BOAT	OM	FERRYMAN

Siddhartha

SAMANAS	CLEVERNESS	BUDDHA	SELF	SEEKING
TIME	DEATH	STONE	GOVINDA	FERRYMAN
OM	BOAT	FREE SPACE	HYPNOTIZES	SIDDHARTHA
EXPERIENCE	BIRD	SON	KAMASWAMI	JETAVANA
KNOWLEDGE	RIVER	HERON	FATHER	TOWNSPEOPLE

Siddhartha

STONE	TIME	WOODS	SIDDHARTHA	HERON
SON	BUDDHA	TEACHERS	FATHER	JETAVANA
KAMASWAMI	TOWNSPEOPLE	FREE SPACE	EXPERIENCE	DICE
OM	GOVINDA	SAMANAS	SEEKING	KNOWLEDGE
SNAKE	BRAHMIN	RIVER	BIRD	FERRYMAN

Siddhartha

HYPNOTIZES	KAMALA	GOTAMA	CLEVERNESS	BOAT
DEATH	SELF	VASUDEVA	FINDING	FERRYMAN
BIRD	RIVER	FREE SPACE	SNAKE	KNOWLEDGE
SEEKING	SAMANAS	GOVINDA	OM	DICE
EXPERIENCE	LOVE	TOWNSPEOPLE	KAMASWAMI	JETAVANA

Siddhartha Vocabulary Word List

No.	Word	Clue/Definition
1.	ALMS	Money, food, or other donations given to the poor
2.	ARDENT	Characterized by intense feeling
3.	ARTISAN	Person skilled in an applied art; craftsman
4.	ASCETICS	Those who renounce material comforts & lead a life of self-discipline
5.	ASSIDUOUS	Constant in effort; working diligently on a task
6.	AUSTERE	Severe in manner or appearance; strict
7.	AVARICIOUS	Immoderately desirous of wealth; greedy
8.	CHASM	Deep cleft in the ground; gorge
9.	COMMUNICABLE	Capable of being easily communicated or transmitted
10.	COMPELLED	Forced or driven to a course of action
11.	CONSIDERATION	Thoughtful or sympathetic regard or respect
12.	COURTESAN	Prostitute or paramour, esp. one associating with noblemen
13.	DAINTY	Pleasing to the taste and often temptingly served or delicate
14.	DECLIVITY	Downward slope
15.	DEFIANCE	Bold resistance to authority or any opposing force
16.	DEMEANOR	Conduct; behavior; attitude
17.	DEVOUT	Pious; religious; devoted to divine worship or service
18.	DISCLOSE	Make known; reveal; uncover
19.	DISILLUSIONMENT	State of being freed from false beliefs
20.	DISPEL	Cause to vanish; get rid of
21.	DIVERSITIES	Points or aspects in which things differ
22.	EMANATED	Flowed out from; came from
23.	ENNUI	Boredom; dissatisfaction resulting from lack of interest
24.	EQUANIMITY	Quality of being calm and even-tempered; composure
25.	ERUDITION	Knowledge acquired by study; learning
26.	ESTEEMED	Respected
27.	EXPIATION	Act of atoning for sins or wrongdoing
28.	FESTER	Infect, inflame, or corrupt
29.	GUILD	Association of tradesmen
30.	HASTINESS	With overly-eager speed and possible carelessness
31.	HINDRANCE	Obstruction; something in the way or a burden
32.	IMPERTURBABLE	Can't be bothered, agitated, or upset
33.	INCIPIENT	Beginning to exist or appear
34.	INDIGNATION	Anger aroused by something unjust, mean, or unworthy
35.	INDOLENT	Inactive; lethargic
36.	INERTIA	Tendency to remain at rest or resist motion or change
37.	INSATIABLE	Incapable of being satisfied or appeased
38.	INTRINSIC	Belonging to a thing by its very nature
39.	IRREFUTABLY	Undeniably; unarguably
40.	LAMENT	Feel or express sorrow or regret
41.	MUTILATE	Injure or disfigure by removing or irreparably damaging parts
42.	ONEROUS	Burdensome; oppressive; troublesome; causing hardship
43.	OSTRACIZED	Excluded from a group
44.	PALLIATIVE	Something that makes pain or sorrow easier to bear
45.	PREDECESSOR	One who came before another in holding an office or position
46.	PRUDENT	Wise or judicious in practical affairs
47.	RENOUNCED	Gave up or put aside voluntarily
48.	SANCTUARY	Sacred or holy place; place of safety
49.	SENILE	Of or belonging to old age or aged persons
50.	SERVILE	Characteristic of, proper to, or customary for slaves

Siddhartha Vocabulary Word List

No.	Word	Clue/Definition
51.	SMARTING	Hurting with a sharp, usually superficial, stinging pain
52.	SOJOURN	Temporary stay; brief period of residence
53.	STRIVE	Try hard
54.	SUBMERGED	Sunk below the surface
55.	TENACIOUS	Persistent; stubborn
56.	TRANSITORY	Not lasting, permanent, or eternal
57.	TRIVIALITIES	Things that are unimportant or frivolous
58.	VENERABLENESS	Quality of commanding respect by virtue of age, character, or position
59.	WRETCHED	Miserable; very unfortunate

Siddhartha Vocabulary Fill In The Blanks 1

_____ 1. Conduct; behavior; attitude

_____ 2. Wise or judicious in practical affairs

_____ 3. Pious; religious; devoted to divine worship or service

_____ 4. Burdensome; oppressive; troublesome; causing hardship

_____ 5. Obstruction; something in the way or a burden

_____ 6. Act of atoning for sins or wrongdoing

_____ 7. Sunk below the surface

_____ 8. Downward slope

_____ 9. Association of tradesmen

_____ 10. Belonging to a thing by its very nature

_____ 11. Persistent; stubborn

_____ 12. Points or aspects in which things differ

_____ 13. Money, food, or other donations given to the poor

_____ 14. Immoderately desirous of wealth; greedy

_____ 15. State of being freed from false beliefs

_____ 16. Person skilled in an applied art; craftsman

_____ 17. Beginning to exist or appear

_____ 18. Undeniably; unarguably

_____ 19. Something that makes pain or sorrow easier to bear

_____ 20. Cause to vanish; get rid of

Siddhartha Vocabulary Fill In The Blanks 1 Answer Key

DEMEANOR	1. Conduct; behavior; attitude
PRUDENT	2. Wise or judicious in practical affairs
DEVOUT	3. Pious; religious; devoted to divine worship or service
ONEROUS	4. Burdensome; oppressive; troublesome; causing hardship
HINDRANCE	5. Obstruction; something in the way or a burden
EXPIATION	6. Act of atoning for sins or wrongdoing
SUBMERGED	7. Sunk below the surface
DECLIVITY	8. Downward slope
GUILD	9. Association of tradesmen
INTRINSIC	10. Belonging to a thing by its very nature
TENACIOUS	11. Persistent; stubborn
DIVERSITIES	12. Points or aspects in which things differ
ALMS	13. Money, food, or other donations given to the poor
AVARICIOUS	14. Immoderately desirous of wealth; greedy
DISILLUSIONMENT	15. State of being freed from false beliefs
ARTISAN	16. Person skilled in an applied art; craftsman
INCIPIENT	17. Beginning to exist or appear
IRREFUTABLY	18. Undeniably; unarguably
PALLIATIVE	19. Something that makes pain or sorrow easier to bear
DISPEL	20. Cause to vanish; get rid of

Siddhartha Vocabulary Fill In The Blanks 2

1. With overly-eager speed and possible carelessness
2. Incapable of being satisfied or appeased
3. Burdensome; oppressive; troublesome; causing hardship
4. Not lasting, permanent, or eternal
5. Inactive; lethargic
6. Boredom; dissatisfaction resulting from lack of interest
7. Person skilled in an applied art; craftsman
8. Conduct; behavior; attitude
9. Association of tradesmen
10. Belonging to a thing by its very nature
11. Something that makes pain or sorrow easier to bear
12. Temporary stay; brief period of residence
13. Wise or judicious in practical affairs
14. Knowledge acquired by study; learning
15. Capable of being easily communicated or transmitted
16. Deep cleft in the ground; gorge
17. Anger aroused by something unjust, mean, or unworthy
18. Sacred or holy place; place of safety
19. Hurting with a sharp, usually superficial, stinging pain
20. Forced or driven to a course of action

Siddhartha Vocabulary Fill In The Blanks 2 Answer Key

HASTINESS	1.	With overly-eager speed and possible carelessness
INSATIABLE	2.	Incapable of being satisfied or appeased
ONEROUS	3.	Burdensome; oppressive; troublesome; causing hardship
TRANSITORY	4.	Not lasting, permanent, or eternal
INDOLENT	5.	Inactive; lethargic
ENNUI	6.	Boredom; dissatisfaction resulting from lack of interest
ARTISAN	7.	Person skilled in an applied art; craftsman
DEMEANOR	8.	Conduct; behavior; attitude
GUILD	9.	Association of tradesmen
INTRINSIC	10.	Belonging to a thing by its very nature
PALLIATIVE	11.	Something that makes pain or sorrow easier to bear
SOJOURN	12.	Temporary stay; brief period of residence
PRUDENT	13.	Wise or judicious in practical affairs
ERUDITION	14.	Knowledge acquired by study; learning
COMMUNICABLE	15.	Capable of being easily communicated or transmitted
CHASM	16.	Deep cleft in the ground; gorge
INDIGNATION	17.	Anger aroused by something unjust, mean, or unworthy
SANCTUARY	18.	Sacred or holy place; place of safety
SMARTING	19.	Hurting with a sharp, usually superficial, stinging pain
COMPELLED	20.	Forced or driven to a course of action

Siddhartha Vocabulary Fill In The Blanks 3

_____ 1. Miserable; very unfortunate

_____ 2. Wise or judicious in practical affairs

_____ 3. Prostitute or paramour, esp. one associating with noblemen

_____ 4. Sunk below the surface

_____ 5. Belonging to a thing by its very nature

_____ 6. Act of atoning for sins or wrongdoing

_____ 7. Injure or disfigure by removing or irreparably damaging parts

_____ 8. Forced or driven to a course of action

_____ 9. Bold resistance to authority or any opposing force

_____ 10. Tendency to remain at rest or resist motion or change

_____ 11. Boredom; dissatisfaction resulting from lack of interest

_____ 12. Thoughtful or sympathetic regard or respect

_____ 13. Severe in manner or appearance; strict

_____ 14. Constant in effort; working diligently on a task

_____ 15. Inactive; lethargic

_____ 16. Try hard

_____ 17. Characterized by intense feeling

_____ 18. Quality of commanding respect by virtue of age, character, or position

_____ 19. Quality of being calm and even-tempered; composure

_____ 20. Conduct; behavior; attitude

Siddhartha Vocabulary Fill In The Blanks 3 Answer Key

WRETCHED	1. Miserable; very unfortunate
PRUDENT	2. Wise or judicious in practical affairs
COURTESAN	3. Prostitute or paramour, esp. one associating with noblemen
SUBMERGED	4. Sunk below the surface
INTRINSIC	5. Belonging to a thing by its very nature
EXPIATION	6. Act of atoning for sins or wrongdoing
MUTILATE	7. Injure or disfigure by removing or irreparably damaging parts
COMPELLED	8. Forced or driven to a course of action
DEFIANCE	9. Bold resistance to authority or any opposing force
INERTIA	10. Tendency to remain at rest or resist motion or change
ENNUI	11. Boredom; dissatisfaction resulting from lack of interest
CONSIDERATION	12. Thoughtful or sympathetic regard or respect
AUSTERE	13. Severe in manner or appearance; strict
ASSIDUOUS	14. Constant in effort; working diligently on a task
INDOLENT	15. Inactive; lethargic
STRIVE	16. Try hard
ARDENT	17. Characterized by intense feeling
VENERABLENESS	18. Quality of commanding respect by virtue of age, character, or position
EQUANIMITY	19. Quality of being calm and even-tempered; composure
DEMEANOR	20. Conduct; behavior; attitude

Siddhartha Vocabulary Fill In The Blanks 4

1. Forced or driven to a course of action
2. Excluded from a group
3. Things that are unimportant or frivolous
4. Belonging to a thing by its very nature
5. Sacred or holy place; place of safety
6. Make known; reveal; uncover
7. With overly-eager speed and possible carelessness
8. Wise or judicious in practical affairs
9. Severe in manner or appearance; strict
10. Quality of commanding respect by virtue of age, character, or position
11. One who came before another in holding an office or position
12. Persistent; stubborn
13. Not lasting, permanent, or eternal
14. Thoughtful or sympathetic regard or respect
15. Miserable; very unfortunate
16. Sunk below the surface
17. Respected
18. Constant in effort; working diligently on a task
19. Pious; religious; devoted to divine worship or service
20. Feel or express sorrow or regret

Siddhartha Vocabulary Fill In The Blanks 4 Answer Key

COMPELLED	1. Forced or driven to a course of action
OSTRACIZED	2. Excluded from a group
TRIVIALITIES	3. Things that are unimportant or frivolous
INTRINSIC	4. Belonging to a thing by its very nature
SANCTUARY	5. Sacred or holy place; place of safety
DISCLOSE	6. Make known; reveal; uncover
HASTINESS	7. With overly-eager speed and possible carelessness
PRUDENT	8. Wise or judicious in practical affairs
AUSTERE	9. Severe in manner or appearance; strict
VENERABLENESS	10. Quality of commanding respect by virtue of age, character, or position
PREDECESSOR	11. One who came before another in holding an office or position
TENACIOUS	12. Persistent; stubborn
TRANSITORY	13. Not lasting, permanent, or eternal
CONSIDERATION	14. Thoughtful or sympathetic regard or respect
WRETCHED	15. Miserable; very unfortunate
SUBMERGED	16. Sunk below the surface
ESTEEMED	17. Respected
ASSIDUOUS	18. Constant in effort; working diligently on a task
DEVOUT	19. Pious; religious; devoted to divine worship or service
LAMENT	20. Feel or express sorrow or regret

Siddhartha Vocabulary Matching 1

___ 1. TRIVIALITIES
___ 2. ONEROUS
___ 3. INCIPIENT
___ 4. COMPELLED
___ 5. DECLIVITY
___ 6. INERTIA
___ 7. SMARTING
___ 8. DISPEL
___ 9. GUILD
___ 10. VENERABLENESS
___ 11. DIVERSITIES
___ 12. INDIGNATION
___ 13. INDOLENT
___ 14. HASTINESS
___ 15. OSTRACIZED
___ 16. DAINTY
___ 17. IRREFUTABLY
___ 18. ASCETICS
___ 19. ASSIDUOUS
___ 20. COMMUNICABLE
___ 21. EMANATED
___ 22. LAMENT
___ 23. SOJOURN
___ 24. TENACIOUS
___ 25. FESTER

A. Excluded from a group
B. Downward slope
C. Persistent; stubborn
D. Inactive; lethargic
E. Pleasing to the taste and often temptingly served or delicate
F. Undeniably; unarguably
G. Constant in effort; working diligently on a task
H. With overly-eager speed and possible carelessness
I. Tendency to remain at rest or resist motion or change
J. Association of tradesmen
K. Burdensome; oppressive; troublesome; causing hardship
L. Flowed out from; came from
M. Hurting with a sharp, usually superficial, stinging pain
N. Things that are unimportant or frivolous
O. Capable of being easily communicated or transmitted
P. Cause to vanish; get rid of
Q. Infect, inflame, or corrupt
R. Temporary stay; brief period of residence
S. Anger aroused by something unjust, mean, or unworthy
T. Quality of commanding respect by virtue of age, character, or position
U. Those who renounce material comforts & lead a life of self-discipline
V. Feel or express sorrow or regret
W. Points or aspects in which things differ
X. Forced or driven to a course of action
Y. Beginning to exist or appear

Siddhartha Vocabulary Matching 1 Answer Key

N - 1. TRIVIALITIES		A. Excluded from a group
K - 2. ONEROUS		B. Downward slope
Y - 3. INCIPIENT		C. Persistent; stubborn
X - 4. COMPELLED		D. Inactive; lethargic
B - 5. DECLIVITY		E. Pleasing to the taste and often temptingly served or delicate
I - 6. INERTIA		F. Undeniably; unarguably
M - 7. SMARTING		G. Constant in effort; working diligently on a task
P - 8. DISPEL		H. With overly-eager speed and possible carelessness
J - 9. GUILD		I. Tendency to remain at rest or resist motion or change
T - 10. VENERABLENESS		J. Association of tradesmen
W - 11. DIVERSITIES		K. Burdensome; oppressive; troublesome; causing hardship
S - 12. INDIGNATION		L. Flowed out from; came from
D - 13. INDOLENT		M. Hurting with a sharp, usually superficial, stinging pain
H - 14. HASTINESS		N. Things that are unimportant or frivolous
A - 15. OSTRACIZED		O. Capable of being easily communicated or transmitted
E - 16. DAINTY		P. Cause to vanish; get rid of
F - 17. IRREFUTABLY		Q. Infect, inflame, or corrupt
U - 18. ASCETICS		R. Temporary stay; brief period of residence
G - 19. ASSIDUOUS		S. Anger aroused by something unjust, mean, or unworthy
O - 20. COMMUNICABLE		T. Quality of commanding respect by virtue of age, character, or position
L - 21. EMANATED		U. Those who renounce material comforts & lead a life of self-discipline
V - 22. LAMENT		V. Feel or express sorrow or regret
R - 23. SOJOURN		W. Points or aspects in which things differ
C - 24. TENACIOUS		X. Forced or driven to a course of action
Q - 25. FESTER		Y. Beginning to exist or appear

Siddhartha Vocabulary Matching 2

___ 1. INDIGNATION
___ 2. TRIVIALITIES
___ 3. ASSIDUOUS
___ 4. MUTILATE
___ 5. CONSIDERATION
___ 6. DAINTY
___ 7. DEVOUT
___ 8. ENNUI
___ 9. INSATIABLE
___ 10. COURTESAN
___ 11. INTRINSIC
___ 12. DISPEL
___ 13. OSTRACIZED
___ 14. TRANSITORY
___ 15. EMANATED
___ 16. INDOLENT
___ 17. AUSTERE
___ 18. WRETCHED
___ 19. EXPIATION
___ 20. ESTEEMED
___ 21. TENACIOUS
___ 22. INERTIA
___ 23. ERUDITION
___ 24. SMARTING
___ 25. PREDECESSOR

A. Injure or disfigure by removing or irreparably damaging parts
B. Knowledge acquired by study; learning
C. Hurting with a sharp, usually superficial, stinging pain
D. Belonging to a thing by its very nature
E. Respected
F. Inactive; lethargic
G. One who came before another in holding an office or position
H. Cause to vanish; get rid of
I. Excluded from a group
J. Miserable; very unfortunate
K. Pleasing to the taste and often temptingly served or delicate
L. Severe in manner or appearance; strict
M. Anger aroused by something unjust, mean, or unworthy
N. Flowed out from; came from
O. Things that are unimportant or frivolous
P. Pious; religious; devoted to divine worship or service
Q. Constant in effort; working diligently on a task
R. Boredom; dissatisfaction resulting from lack of interest
S. Not lasting, permanent, or eternal
T. Prostitute or paramour, esp. one associating with noblemen
U. Act of atoning for sins or wrongdoing
V. Incapable of being satisfied or appeased
W. Tendency to remain at rest or resist motion or change
X. Persistent; stubborn
Y. Thoughtful or sympathetic regard or respect

Siddhartha Vocabulary Matching 2 Answer Key

M - 1. INDIGNATION		A. Injure or disfigure by removing or irreparably damaging parts
O - 2. TRIVIALITIES		B. Knowledge acquired by study; learning
Q - 3. ASSIDUOUS		C. Hurting with a sharp, usually superficial, stinging pain
A - 4. MUTILATE		D. Belonging to a thing by its very nature
Y - 5. CONSIDERATION		E. Respected
K - 6. DAINTY		F. Inactive; lethargic
P - 7. DEVOUT		G. One who came before another in holding an office or position
R - 8. ENNUI		H. Cause to vanish; get rid of
V - 9. INSATIABLE		I. Excluded from a group
T - 10. COURTESAN		J. Miserable; very unfortunate
D - 11. INTRINSIC		K. Pleasing to the taste and often temptingly served or delicate
H - 12. DISPEL		L. Severe in manner or appearance; strict
I - 13. OSTRACIZED		M. Anger aroused by something unjust, mean, or unworthy
S - 14. TRANSITORY		N. Flowed out from; came from
N - 15. EMANATED		O. Things that are unimportant or frivolous
F - 16. INDOLENT		P. Pious; religious; devoted to divine worship or service
L - 17. AUSTERE		Q. Constant in effort; working diligently on a task
J - 18. WRETCHED		R. Boredom; dissatisfaction resulting from lack of interest
U - 19. EXPIATION		S. Not lasting, permanent, or eternal
E - 20. ESTEEMED		T. Prostitute or paramour, esp. one associating with noblemen
X - 21. TENACIOUS		U. Act of atoning for sins or wrongdoing
W - 22. INERTIA		V. Incapable of being satisfied or appeased
B - 23. ERUDITION		W. Tendency to remain at rest or resist motion or change
C - 24. SMARTING		X. Persistent; stubborn
G - 25. PREDECESSOR		Y. Thoughtful or sympathetic regard or respect

Siddhartha Vocabulary Matching 3

___ 1. DEFIANCE
___ 2. INDIGNATION
___ 3. SANCTUARY
___ 4. HINDRANCE
___ 5. SOJOURN
___ 6. INTRINSIC
___ 7. IRREFUTABLY
___ 8. PRUDENT
___ 9. ASCETICS
___ 10. OSTRACIZED
___ 11. ARDENT
___ 12. DEMEANOR
___ 13. COURTESAN
___ 14. RENOUNCED
___ 15. INERTIA
___ 16. DIVERSITIES
___ 17. STRIVE
___ 18. DISILLUSIONMENT
___ 19. CONSIDERATION
___ 20. PREDECESSOR
___ 21. ALMS
___ 22. PALLIATIVE
___ 23. INCIPIENT
___ 24. EQUANIMITY
___ 25. INSATIABLE

A. Sacred or holy place; place of safety
B. Anger aroused by something unjust, mean, or unworthy
C. Money, food, or other donations given to the poor
D. Try hard
E. Temporary stay; brief period of residence
F. Belonging to a thing by its very nature
G. Excluded from a group
H. Incapable of being satisfied or appeased
I. Conduct; behavior; attitude
J. Beginning to exist or appear
K. Quality of being calm and even-tempered; composure
L. One who came before another in holding an office or position
M. Obstruction; something in the way or a burden
N. Points or aspects in which things differ
O. Prostitute or paramour, esp. one associating with noblemen
P. Undeniably; unarguably
Q. Bold resistance to authority or any opposing force
R. Wise or judicious in practical affairs
S. Something that makes pain or sorrow easier to bear
T. Thoughtful or sympathetic regard or respect
U. Gave up or put aside voluntarily
V. Those who renounce material comforts & lead a life of self-discipline
W. Characterized by intense feeling
X. Tendency to remain at rest or resist motion or change
Y. State of being freed from false beliefs

Siddhartha Vocabulary Matching 3 Answer Key

Q - 1.	DEFIANCE	A.	Sacred or holy place; place of safety
B - 2.	INDIGNATION	B.	Anger aroused by something unjust, mean, or unworthy
A - 3.	SANCTUARY	C.	Money, food, or other donations given to the poor
M - 4.	HINDRANCE	D.	Try hard
E - 5.	SOJOURN	E.	Temporary stay; brief period of residence
F - 6.	INTRINSIC	F.	Belonging to a thing by its very nature
P - 7.	IRREFUTABLY	G.	Excluded from a group
R - 8.	PRUDENT	H.	Incapable of being satisfied or appeased
V - 9.	ASCETICS	I.	Conduct; behavior; attitude
G - 10.	OSTRACIZED	J.	Beginning to exist or appear
W - 11.	ARDENT	K.	Quality of being calm and even-tempered; composure
I - 12.	DEMEANOR	L.	One who came before another in holding an office or position
O - 13.	COURTESAN	M.	Obstruction; something in the way or a burden
U - 14.	RENOUNCED	N.	Points or aspects in which things differ
X - 15.	INERTIA	O.	Prostitute or paramour, esp. one associating with noblemen
N - 16.	DIVERSITIES	P.	Undeniably; unarguably
D - 17.	STRIVE	Q.	Bold resistance to authority or any opposing force
Y - 18.	DISILLUSIONMENT	R.	Wise or judicious in practical affairs
T - 19.	CONSIDERATION	S.	Something that makes pain or sorrow easier to bear
L - 20.	PREDECESSOR	T.	Thoughtful or sympathetic regard or respect
C - 21.	ALMS	U.	Gave up or put aside voluntarily
S - 22.	PALLIATIVE	V.	Those who renounce material comforts & lead a life of self-discipline
J - 23.	INCIPIENT	W.	Characterized by intense feeling
K - 24.	EQUANIMITY	X.	Tendency to remain at rest or resist motion or change
H - 25.	INSATIABLE	Y.	State of being freed from false beliefs

Siddhartha Vocabulary Matching 4

___ 1. DAINTY
___ 2. COMMUNICABLE
___ 3. PRUDENT
___ 4. EXPIATION
___ 5. DEVOUT
___ 6. ARDENT
___ 7. TENACIOUS
___ 8. STRIVE
___ 9. ASSIDUOUS
___ 10. COMPELLED
___ 11. EQUANIMITY
___ 12. GUILD
___ 13. COURTESAN
___ 14. AUSTERE
___ 15. INERTIA
___ 16. LAMENT
___ 17. RENOUNCED
___ 18. ENNUI
___ 19. ESTEEMED
___ 20. ALMS
___ 21. ARTISAN
___ 22. HINDRANCE
___ 23. FESTER
___ 24. SANCTUARY
___ 25. IMPERTURBABLE

A. Feel or express sorrow or regret
B. Tendency to remain at rest or resist motion or change
C. Forced or driven to a course of action
D. Severe in manner or appearance; strict
E. Infect, inflame, or corrupt
F. Pious; religious; devoted to divine worship or service
G. Money, food, or other donations given to the poor
H. Can't be bothered, agitated, or upset
I. Wise or judicious in practical affairs
J. Gave up or put aside voluntarily
K. Act of atoning for sins or wrongdoing
L. Try hard
M. Prostitute or paramour, esp. one associating with noblemen
N. Sacred or holy place; place of safety
O. Characterized by intense feeling
P. Quality of being calm and even-tempered; composure
Q. Boredom; dissatisfaction resulting from lack of interest
R. Capable of being easily communicated or transmitted
S. Persistent; stubborn
T. Person skilled in an applied art; craftsman
U. Obstruction; something in the way or a burden
V. Respected
W. Pleasing to the taste and often temptingly served or delicate
X. Constant in effort; working diligently on a task
Y. Association of tradesmen

Siddhartha Vocabulary Matching 4 Answer Key

W - 1. DAINTY		A. Feel or express sorrow or regret
R - 2. COMMUNICABLE		B. Tendency to remain at rest or resist motion or change
I - 3. PRUDENT		C. Forced or driven to a course of action
K - 4. EXPIATION		D. Severe in manner or appearance; strict
F - 5. DEVOUT		E. Infect, inflame, or corrupt
O - 6. ARDENT		F. Pious; religious; devoted to divine worship or service
S - 7. TENACIOUS		G. Money, food, or other donations given to the poor
L - 8. STRIVE		H. Can't be bothered, agitated, or upset
X - 9. ASSIDUOUS		I. Wise or judicious in practical affairs
C - 10. COMPELLED		J. Gave up or put aside voluntarily
P - 11. EQUANIMITY		K. Act of atoning for sins or wrongdoing
Y - 12. GUILD		L. Try hard
M - 13. COURTESAN		M. Prostitute or paramour, esp. one associating with noblemen
D - 14. AUSTERE		N. Sacred or holy place; place of safety
B - 15. INERTIA		O. Characterized by intense feeling
A - 16. LAMENT		P. Quality of being calm and even-tempered; composure
J - 17. RENOUNCED		Q. Boredom; dissatisfaction resulting from lack of interest
Q - 18. ENNUI		R. Capable of being easily communicated or transmitted
V - 19. ESTEEMED		S. Persistent; stubborn
G - 20. ALMS		T. Person skilled in an applied art; craftsman
T - 21. ARTISAN		U. Obstruction; something in the way or a burden
U - 22. HINDRANCE		V. Respected
E - 23. FESTER		W. Pleasing to the taste and often temptingly served or delicate
N - 24. SANCTUARY		X. Constant in effort; working diligently on a task
H - 25. IMPERTURBABLE		Y. Association of tradesmen

Siddhartha Vocabulary Magic Squares 1

Match the definition with the vocabulary word. Put your answers in the magic squares below. When your answers are correct, all columns and rows will add to the same number.

A. LAMENT
B. COURTESAN
C. AVARICIOUS
D. SOJOURN
E. SMARTING
F. INCIPIENT
G. INTRINSIC
H. COMPELLED
I. STRIVE
J. PREDECESSOR
K. FESTER
L. DISCLOSE
M. SERVILE
N. ARDENT
O. EQUANIMITY
P. INERTIA

1. Forced or driven to a course of action
2. Characteristic of, proper to, or customary for slaves
3. Prostitute or paramour, esp. one associating with noblemen
4. Infect, inflame, or corrupt
5. One who came before another in holding an office or position
6. Immoderately desirous of wealth; greedy
7. Tendency to remain at rest or resist motion or change
8. Hurting with a sharp, usually superficial, stinging pain
9. Quality of being calm and even-tempered; composure
10. Beginning to exist or appear
11. Try hard
12. Temporary stay; brief period of residence
13. Feel or express sorrow or regret
14. Make known; reveal; uncover
15. Belonging to a thing by its very nature
16. Characterized by intense feeling

A=	B=	C=	D=
E=	F=	G=	H=
I=	J=	K=	L=
M=	N=	O=	P=

Siddhartha Vocabulary Magic Squares 1 Answer Key

Match the definition with the vocabulary word. Put your answers in the magic squares below. When your answers are correct, all columns and rows will add to the same number.

A. LAMENT
B. COURTESAN
C. AVARICIOUS
D. SOJOURN
E. SMARTING
F. INCIPIENT
G. INTRINSIC
H. COMPELLED
I. STRIVE
J. PREDECESSOR
K. FESTER
L. DISCLOSE
M. SERVILE
N. ARDENT
O. EQUANIMITY
P. INERTIA

1. Forced or driven to a course of action
2. Characteristic of, proper to, or customary for slaves
3. Prostitute or paramour, esp. one associating with noblemen
4. Infect, inflame, or corrupt
5. One who came before another in holding an office or position
6. Immoderately desirous of wealth; greedy
7. Tendency to remain at rest or resist motion or change
8. Hurting with a sharp, usually superficial, stinging pain
9. Quality of being calm and even-tempered; composure
10. Beginning to exist or appear
11. Try hard
12. Temporary stay; brief period of residence
13. Feel or express sorrow or regret
14. Make known; reveal; uncover
15. Belonging to a thing by its very nature
16. Characterized by intense feeling

A=13	B=3	C=6	D=12
E=8	F=10	G=15	H=1
I=11	J=5	K=4	L=14
M=2	N=16	O=9	P=7

Siddhartha Vocabulary Magic Squares 2

Match the definition with the vocabulary word. Put your answers in the magic squares below. When your answers are correct, all columns and rows will add to the same number.

A. ALMS
B. RENOUNCED
C. DEMEANOR
D. COMPELLED
E. SMARTING
F. COURTESAN
G. OSTRACIZED
H. EXPIATION
I. EQUANIMITY
J. ARDENT
K. DIVERSITIES
L. ENNUI
M. STRIVE
N. ONEROUS
O. LAMENT
P. SANCTUARY

1. Feel or express sorrow or regret
2. Forced or driven to a course of action
3. Characterized by intense feeling
4. Hurting with a sharp, usually superficial, stinging pain
5. Quality of being calm and even-tempered; composure
6. Prostitute or paramour, esp. one associating with noblemen
7. Sacred or holy place; place of safety
8. Conduct; behavior; attitude
9. Act of atoning for sins or wrongdoing
10. Points or aspects in which things differ
11. Money, food, or other donations given to the poor
12. Burdensome; oppressive; troublesome; causing hardship
13. Gave up or put aside voluntarily
14. Try hard
15. Excluded from a group
16. Boredom; dissatisfaction resulting from lack of interest

A=	B=	C=	D=
E=	F=	G=	H=
I=	J=	K=	L=
M=	N=	O=	P=

Siddhartha Vocabulary Magic Squares 2 Answer Key

Match the definition with the vocabulary word. Put your answers in the magic squares below. When your answers are correct, all columns and rows will add to the same number.

A. ALMS
B. RENOUNCED
C. DEMEANOR
D. COMPELLED
E. SMARTING
F. COURTESAN
G. OSTRACIZED
H. EXPIATION
I. EQUANIMITY
J. ARDENT
K. DIVERSITIES
L. ENNUI
M. STRIVE
N. ONEROUS
O. LAMENT
P. SANCTUARY

1. Feel or express sorrow or regret
2. Forced or driven to a course of action
3. Characterized by intense feeling
4. Hurting with a sharp, usually superficial, stinging pain
5. Quality of being calm and even-tempered; composure
6. Prostitute or paramour, esp. one associating with noblemen
7. Sacred or holy place; place of safety
8. Conduct; behavior; attitude
9. Act of atoning for sins or wrongdoing
10. Points or aspects in which things differ
11. Money, food, or other donations given to the poor
12. Burdensome; oppressive; troublesome; causing hardship
13. Gave up or put aside voluntarily
14. Try hard
15. Excluded from a group
16. Boredom; dissatisfaction resulting from lack of interest

A=11	B=13	C=8	D=2
E=4	F=6	G=15	H=9
I=5	J=3	K=10	L=16
M=14	N=12	O=1	P=7

Siddhartha Vocabulary Magic Squares 3

Match the definition with the vocabulary word. Put your answers in the magic squares below. When your answers are correct, all columns and rows will add to the same number.

A. RENOUNCED
B. STRIVE
C. DISPEL
D. TRIVIALITIES
E. DISILLUSIONMENT
F. SANCTUARY
G. FESTER
H. GUILD
I. PALLIATIVE
J. CHASM
K. SUBMERGED
L. EQUANIMITY
M. EXPIATION
N. ENNUI
O. VENERABLENESS
P. ERUDITION

1. Gave up or put aside voluntarily
2. Boredom; dissatisfaction resulting from lack of interest
3. Deep cleft in the ground; gorge
4. State of being freed from false beliefs
5. Infect, inflame, or corrupt
6. Quality of being calm and even-tempered; composure
7. Knowledge acquired by study; learning
8. Cause to vanish; get rid of
9. Quality of commanding respect by virtue of age, character, or position
10. Things that are unimportant or frivolous
11. Association of tradesmen
12. Sunk below the surface
13. Something that makes pain or sorrow easier to bear
14. Sacred or holy place; place of safety
15. Try hard
16. Act of atoning for sins or wrongdoing

A=	B=	C=	D=
E=	F=	G=	H=
I=	J=	K=	L=
M=	N=	O=	P=

Siddhartha Vocabulary Magic Squares 3 Answer Key

Match the definition with the vocabulary word. Put your answers in the magic squares below. When your answers are correct, all columns and rows will add to the same number.

A. RENOUNCED
B. STRIVE
C. DISPEL
D. TRIVIALITIES
E. DISILLUSIONMENT
F. SANCTUARY
G. FESTER
H. GUILD
I. PALLIATIVE
J. CHASM
K. SUBMERGED
L. EQUANIMITY
M. EXPIATION
N. ENNUI
O. VENERABLENESS
P. ERUDITION

1. Gave up or put aside voluntarily
2. Boredom; dissatisfaction resulting from lack of interest
3. Deep cleft in the ground; gorge
4. State of being freed from false beliefs
5. Infect, inflame, or corrupt
6. Quality of being calm and even-tempered; composure
7. Knowledge acquired by study; learning
8. Cause to vanish; get rid of
9. Quality of commanding respect by virtue of age, character, or position
10. Things that are unimportant or frivolous
11. Association of tradesmen
12. Sunk below the surface
13. Something that makes pain or sorrow easier to bear
14. Sacred or holy place; place of safety
15. Try hard
16. Act of atoning for sins or wrongdoing

A=1	B=15	C=8	D=10
E=4	F=14	G=5	H=11
I=13	J=3	K=12	L=6
M=16	N=2	O=9	P=7

Siddhartha Vocabulary Magic Squares 4

Match the definition with the vocabulary word. Put your answers in the magic squares below. When your answers are correct, all columns and rows will add to the same number.

A. DISCLOSE
B. IMPERTURBABLE
C. TENACIOUS
D. ENNUI
E. MUTILATE
F. PALLIATIVE
G. AUSTERE
H. DIVERSITIES
I. SMARTING
J. SERVILE
K. ASSIDUOUS
L. INDIGNATION
M. EMANATED
N. DAINTY
O. LAMENT
P. EXPIATION

1. Persistent; stubborn
2. Characteristic of, proper to, or customary for slaves
3. Something that makes pain or sorrow easier to bear
4. Feel or express sorrow or regret
5. Act of atoning for sins or wrongdoing
6. Injure or disfigure by removing or irreparably damaging parts
7. Hurting with a sharp, usually superficial, stinging pain
8. Boredom; dissatisfaction resulting from lack of interest
9. Flowed out from; came from
10. Points or aspects in which things differ
11. Anger aroused by something unjust, mean, or unworthy
12. Make known; reveal; uncover
13. Can't be bothered, agitated, or upset
14. Constant in effort; working diligently on a task
15. Severe in manner or appearance; strict
16. Pleasing to the taste and often temptingly served or delicate

A=	B=	C=	D=
E=	F=	G=	H=
I=	J=	K=	L=
M=	N=	O=	P=

Siddhartha Vocabulary Magic Squares 4 Answer Key

Match the definition with the vocabulary word. Put your answers in the magic squares below. When your answers are correct, all columns and rows will add to the same number.

A. DISCLOSE
B. IMPERTURBABLE
C. TENACIOUS
D. ENNUI
E. MUTILATE
F. PALLIATIVE
G. AUSTERE
H. DIVERSITIES
I. SMARTING
J. SERVILE
K. ASSIDUOUS
L. INDIGNATION
M. EMANATED
N. DAINTY
O. LAMENT
P. EXPIATION

1. Persistent; stubborn
2. Characteristic of, proper to, or customary for slaves
3. Something that makes pain or sorrow easier to bear
4. Feel or express sorrow or regret
5. Act of atoning for sins or wrongdoing
6. Injure or disfigure by removing or irreparably damaging parts
7. Hurting with a sharp, usually superficial, stinging pain
8. Boredom; dissatisfaction resulting from lack of interest
9. Flowed out from; came from
10. Points or aspects in which things differ
11. Anger aroused by something unjust, mean, or unworthy
12. Make known; reveal; uncover
13. Can't be bothered, agitated, or upset
14. Constant in effort; working diligently on a task
15. Severe in manner or appearance; strict
16. Pleasing to the taste and often temptingly served or delicate

A=12	B=13	C=1	D=8
E=6	F=3	G=15	H=10
I=7	J=2	K=14	L=11
M=9	N=16	O=4	P=5

Siddhartha Vocabulary Juggle Letters 1

1. LAMS = 1. _____
Money, food, or other donations given to the poor

2. ISIETESIRVD = 2. _____
Points or aspects in which things differ

3. CTEAISSC = 3. _____
Those who renounce material comforts & lead a life of self-discipline

4. YANITTOSRR = 4. _____
Not lasting, permanent, or eternal

5. LEIRPMTEBAUBR = 5. _____
Can't be bothered, agitated, or upset

6. NOLNTDIE = 6. _____
Inactive; lethargic

7. EDFCNEAI = 7. _____
Bold resistance to authority or any opposing force

8. EGURSEMBD = 8. _____
Sunk below the surface

9. NTEMAEAD = 9. _____
Flowed out from; came from

10. AFBILRTEUYR =10. _____
Undeniably; unarguably

11. IRVIESIITTAL =11. _____
Things that are unimportant or frivolous

12. UNSOROJ =12. _____
Temporary stay; brief period of residence

13. IAMTETUL =13. _____
Injure or disfigure by removing or irreparably damaging parts

14. ATRGMINS =14. _____
Hurting with a sharp, usually superficial, stinging pain

Siddhartha Vocabulary Juggle Letters 1 Answer Key

1. LAMS = 1. ALMS
   Money, food, or other donations given to the poor

2. ISIETESIRVD = 2. DIVERSITIES
   Points or aspects in which things differ

3. CTEAISSC = 3. ASCETICS
   Those who renounce material comforts & lead a life of self-discipline

4. YANITTOSRR = 4. TRANSITORY
   Not lasting, permanent, or eternal

5. LEIRPMTEBAUBR = 5. IMPERTURBABLE
   Can't be bothered, agitated, or upset

6. NOLNTDIE = 6. INDOLENT
   Inactive; lethargic

7. EDFCNEAI = 7. DEFIANCE
   Bold resistance to authority or any opposing force

8. EGURSEMBD = 8. SUBMERGED
   Sunk below the surface

9. NTEMAEAD = 9. EMANATED
   Flowed out from; came from

10. AFBILRTEUYR = 10. IRREFUTABLY
    Undeniably; unarguably

11. IRVIESIITTAL = 11. TRIVIALITIES
    Things that are unimportant or frivolous

12. UNSOROJ = 12. SOJOURN
    Temporary stay; brief period of residence

13. IAMTETUL = 13. MUTILATE
    Injure or disfigure by removing or irreparably damaging parts

14. ATRGMINS = 14. SMARTING
    Hurting with a sharp, usually superficial, stinging pain

Siddhartha Vocabulary Juggle Letters 2

1. TPDRNEU = 1. _____
   Wise or judicious in practical affairs

2. NOIIANNTGID = 2. _____
   Anger aroused by something unjust, mean, or unworthy

3. NNITEPIIC = 3. _____
   Beginning to exist or appear

4. SCIASECT = 4. _____
   Those who renounce material comforts & lead a life of self-discipline

5. AAITVLILPE = 5. _____
   Something that makes pain or sorrow easier to bear

6. IUDUAOSSS = 6. _____
   Constant in effort; working diligently on a task

7. OISCLSED = 7. _____
   Make known; reveal; uncover

8. CDUNENERO = 8. _____
   Gave up or put aside voluntarily

9. AEENTADM = 9. _____
   Flowed out from; came from

10. NYOTRATIRS = 10. _____
    Not lasting, permanent, or eternal

11. NTAIDY = 11. _____
    Pleasing to the taste and often temptingly served or delicate

12. ACSHM = 12. _____
    Deep cleft in the ground; gorge

13. HETCREDW = 13. _____
    Miserable; very unfortunate

14. ERHNADICN = 14. _____
    Obstruction; something in the way or a burden

Siddhartha Vocabulary Juggle Letters 2 Answer Key

1. TPDRNEU = 1. PRUDENT
   Wise or judicious in practical affairs

2. NOIIANNTGID = 2. INDIGNATION
   Anger aroused by something unjust, mean, or unworthy

3. NNITEPIIC = 3. INCIPIENT
   Beginning to exist or appear

4. SCIASECT = 4. ASCETICS
   Those who renounce material comforts & lead a life of self-discipline

5. AAITVLILPE = 5. PALLIATIVE
   Something that makes pain or sorrow easier to bear

6. IUDUAOSSS = 6. ASSIDUOUS
   Constant in effort; working diligently on a task

7. OISCLSED = 7. DISCLOSE
   Make known; reveal; uncover

8. CDUNENERO = 8. RENOUNCED
   Gave up or put aside voluntarily

9. AEENTADM = 9. EMANATED
   Flowed out from; came from

10. NYOTRATIRS =10. TRANSITORY
    Not lasting, permanent, or eternal

11. NTAIDY =11. DAINTY
    Pleasing to the taste and often temptingly served or delicate

12. ACSHM =12. CHASM
    Deep cleft in the ground; gorge

13. HETCREDW =13. WRETCHED
    Miserable; very unfortunate

14. ERHNADICN =14. HINDRANCE
    Obstruction; something in the way or a burden

Siddhartha Vocabulary Juggle Letters 3

1. IENNCADHR = 1. _____
   Obstruction; something in the way or a burden

2. MHSCA = 2. _____
   Deep cleft in the ground; gorge

3. TMNLEA = 3. _____
   Feel or express sorrow or regret

4. EREMBDSUG = 4. _____
   Sunk below the surface

5. ENUOROS = 5. _____
   Burdensome; oppressive; troublesome; causing hardship

6. NAAEMETD = 6. _____
   Flowed out from; came from

7. SLMA = 7. _____
   Money, food, or other donations given to the poor

8. RNCOSTNEIOAID = 8. _____
   Thoughtful or sympathetic regard or respect

9. ACRSNATYU = 9. _____
   Sacred or holy place; place of safety

10. ITNMQYEUAI = 10. _____
    Quality of being calm and even-tempered; composure

11. TCAOEIUSN = 11. _____
    Persistent; stubborn

12. RLANSVEESENBE = 12. _____
    Quality of commanding respect by virtue of age, character, or position

13. ERTEUAS = 13. _____
    Severe in manner or appearance; strict

14. NOEDTNLI = 14. _____
    Inactive; lethargic

Siddhartha Vocabulary Juggle Letters 3 Answer Key

1. IENNCADHR = 1. HINDRANCE
   Obstruction; something in the way or a burden

2. MHSCA = 2. CHASM
   Deep cleft in the ground; gorge

3. TMNLEA = 3. LAMENT
   Feel or express sorrow or regret

4. EREMBDSUG = 4. SUBMERGED
   Sunk below the surface

5. ENUOROS = 5. ONEROUS
   Burdensome; oppressive; troublesome; causing hardship

6. NAAEMETD = 6. EMANATED
   Flowed out from; came from

7. SLMA = 7. ALMS
   Money, food, or other donations given to the poor

8. RNCOSTNEIOAID = 8. CONSIDERATION
   Thoughtful or sympathetic regard or respect

9. ACRSNATYU = 9. SANCTUARY
   Sacred or holy place; place of safety

10. ITNMQYEUAI =10. EQUANIMITY
    Quality of being calm and even-tempered; composure

11. TCAOEIUSN =11. TENACIOUS
    Persistent; stubborn

12. RLANSVEESENBE =12. VENERABLENESS
    Quality of commanding respect by virtue of age, character, or position

13. ERTEUAS =13. AUSTERE
    Severe in manner or appearance; strict

14. NOEDTNLI =14. INDOLENT
    Inactive; lethargic

Siddhartha Vocabulary Juggle Letters 4

1. RFESET = 1. _____
Infect, inflame, or corrupt

2. ULDIG = 2. _____
Association of tradesmen

3. SINIIRTNC = 3. _____
Belonging to a thing by its very nature

4. TSDIEIRIESV = 4. _____
Points or aspects in which things differ

5. EMSEEETD = 5. _____
Respected

6. ENEFDIAC = 6. _____
Bold resistance to authority or any opposing force

7. ERLESVI = 7. _____
Characteristic of, proper to, or customary for slaves

8. ATNILASBEI = 8. _____
Incapable of being satisfied or appeased

9. NCIIPTNEI = 9. _____
Beginning to exist or appear

10. PISLED = 10. _____
Cause to vanish; get rid of

11. LSMA = 11. _____
Money, food, or other donations given to the poor

12. EPEOCMDLL = 12. _____
Forced or driven to a course of action

13. VISRTE = 13. _____
Try hard

14. ESEEOSDRRPC = 14. _____
One who came before another in holding an office or position

Siddhartha Vocabulary Juggle Letters 4 Answer Key

1. RFESET = 1. FESTER
   Infect, inflame, or corrupt

2. ULDIG = 2. GUILD
   Association of tradesmen

3. SINIIRTNC = 3. INTRINSIC
   Belonging to a thing by its very nature

4. TSDIEIRIESV = 4. DIVERSITIES
   Points or aspects in which things differ

5. EMSEEETD = 5. ESTEEMED
   Respected

6. ENEFDIAC = 6. DEFIANCE
   Bold resistance to authority or any opposing force

7. ERLESVI = 7. SERVILE
   Characteristic of, proper to, or customary for slaves

8. ATNILASBEI = 8. INSATIABLE
   Incapable of being satisfied or appeased

9. NCIIPTNEI = 9. INCIPIENT
   Beginning to exist or appear

10. PISLED =10. DISPEL
    Cause to vanish; get rid of

11. LSMA =11. ALMS
    Money, food, or other donations given to the poor

12. EPEOCMDLL =12. COMPELLED
    Forced or driven to a course of action

13. VISRTE =13. STRIVE
    Try hard

14. ESEEOSDRRPC =14. PREDECESSOR
    One who came before another in holding an office or position

Siddhartha Vocabulary Word Search 1

```
A R T I S A N W R E T C H E D E C L D
G D C A C M L G C E Y N I S R L E A C
U E O R I C A W F C N N C E D I L M X
I M M D T W P R K B C N T R E N B E H
L E M E E E R D T I W S U V V E A N Z
D A U N C Q U A P I U G X I O S B T N
P N N T S U D I G A N F P L U Z R R Q
Z O I N A A E N T M F G I E T I U E T
T R C E M N N T R U M E N F V N T N W
E K A L T I T Y N T H R S I Y D R O C
N D B O L M N E G I N B A T B D E U F
A S L D B I S E N L Z L T D E G P N S
C T E N Z T K D R A I N I T I R M C M
I R S I E Y R A U T C N A S H S I E G
O I V E H A C Q I E I N B L K S P D F
U V M H N K F E V T A A L M M F L E Y
S E T C H A S M D M D B E R R S M D L
D M E M C I R R E F U T A B L Y Y G P
```

Association of tradesmen (5)
Beginning to exist or appear (9)
Boredom; dissatisfaction resulting from lack of interest (5)
Can't be bothered, agitated, or upset (13)
Capable of being easily communicated or transmitted (12)
Cause to vanish; get rid of (6)
Characteristic of, proper to, or customary for slaves (7)
Characterized by intense feeling (6)
Conduct; behavior; attitude (8)
Deep cleft in the ground; gorge (5)
Feel or express sorrow or regret (6)
Flowed out from; came from (8)
Gave up or put aside voluntarily (9)
Hurting with a sharp, usually superficial, stinging pain (8)
Inactive; lethargic (8)
Incapable of being satisfied or appeased (10)
Infect, inflame, or corrupt (6)
Injure or disfigure by removing or irreparably damaging parts (8)
Miserable; very unfortunate (8)
Money, food, or other donations given to the poor (4)
Obstruction; something in the way or a burden (9)
Of or belonging to old age or aged persons (6)
Persistent; stubborn (9)
Person skilled in an applied art; craftsman (7)
Pious; religious; devoted to divine worship or service (6)
Pleasing to the taste and often temptingly served or delicate (6)
Quality of being calm and even-tempered; composure (10)
Respected (8)
Sacred or holy place; place of safety (9)
Severe in manner or appearance; strict (7)
Tendency to remain at rest or resist motion or change (7)
Things that are unimportant or frivolous (12)
Those who renounce material comforts & lead a life of self-discipline (8)
Try hard (6)
Undeniably; unarguably (11)
Wise or judicious in practical affairs (7)

Siddhartha Vocabulary Word Search 1 Answer Key

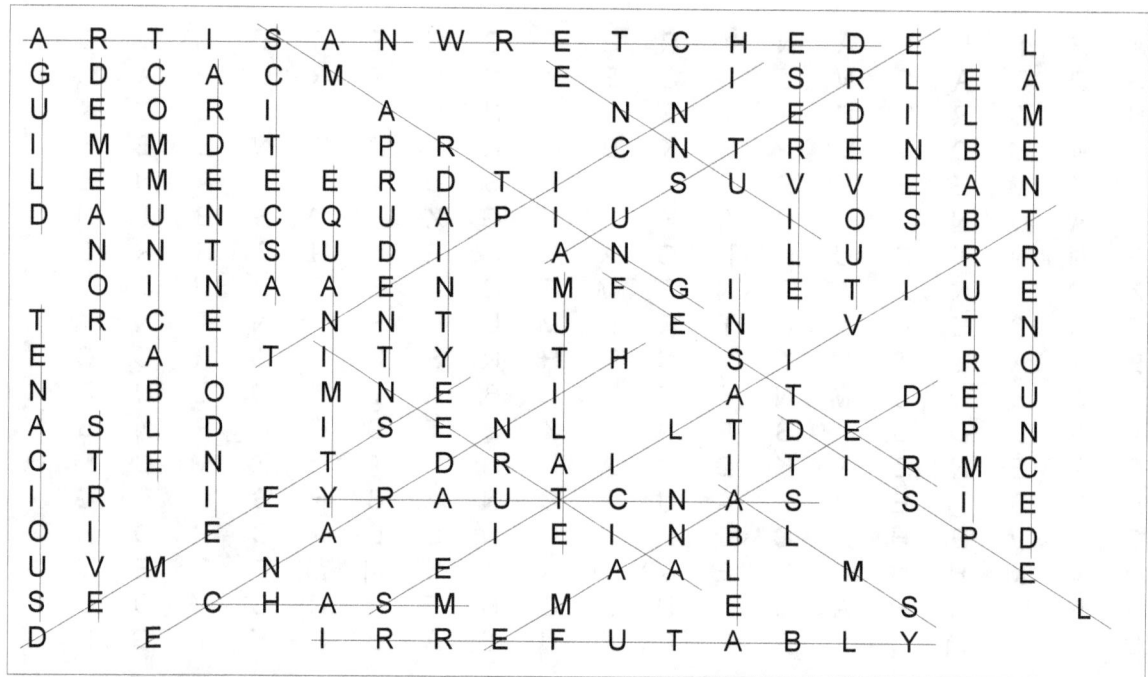

Association of tradesmen (5)
Beginning to exist or appear (9)
Boredom; dissatisfaction resulting from lack of interest (5)
Can't be bothered, agitated, or upset (13)
Capable of being easily communicated or transmitted (12)
Cause to vanish; get rid of (6)
Characteristic of, proper to, or customary for slaves (7)
Characterized by intense feeling (6)
Conduct; behavior; attitude (8)
Deep cleft in the ground; gorge (5)
Feel or express sorrow or regret (6)
Flowed out from; came from (8)
Gave up or put aside voluntarily (9)
Hurting with a sharp, usually superficial, stinging pain (8)
Inactive; lethargic (8)
Incapable of being satisfied or appeased (10)
Infect, inflame, or corrupt (6)
Injure or disfigure by removing or irreparably damaging parts (8)
Miserable; very unfortunate (8)
Money, food, or other donations given to the poor (4)
Obstruction; something in the way or a burden (9)
Of or belonging to old age or aged persons (6)
Persistent; stubborn (9)
Person skilled in an applied art; craftsman (7)
Pious; religious; devoted to divine worship or service (6)
Pleasing to the taste and often temptingly served or delicate (6)
Quality of being calm and even-tempered; composure (10)
Respected (8)
Sacred or holy place; place of safety (9)
Severe in manner or appearance; strict (7)
Tendency to remain at rest or resist motion or change (7)
Things that are unimportant or frivolous (12)
Those who renounce material comforts & lead a life of self-discipline (8)
Try hard (6)
Undeniably; unarguably (11)
Wise or judicious in practical affairs (7)

Siddhartha Vocabulary Word Search 2

```
A L M S A N C T U A R Y T N E D U R P
R M I E O C H A S M X L W T X D T H D
T U N N F J R Z E N S B S Y P B S N R
I T D I E X O Z V F H A S T I N E S S
S I I L S V N U I K Y T N I A D R R L
A L G E T S A X R N D U C G T C V K T
N A N L E E S T N E F J X I M I E B
W T A D R I M D S H T E P Q O P L Z K
R E T Y D T E E A Y A R G F N B E R G
E M I T Y I D Z R V N R B U A T K E C
T G O I A L S I F Z A I D C I E Y N C
C K N V I A L C J Z M R I Q S L Z O X
H T V I T I J A L Z E N I T C D D U N
E N H L R V Z R X O U F E C C E S N F
D E S C E I C T D M S E V N I V M C G
V D B E N R Y S M L M E V J N O Y E V
E R U D I T I O N E R O U S G U U D Z
L A M E N T C G D I S P E L Z T I S Q
```

Act of atoning for sins or wrongdoing (9)
Anger aroused by something unjust, mean, or unworthy (11)
Association of tradesmen (5)
Boredom; dissatisfaction resulting from lack of interest (5)
Burdensome; oppressive; troublesome; causing hardship (7)
Capable of being easily communicated or transmitted (12)
Cause to vanish; get rid of (6)
Characteristic of, proper to, or customary for slaves (7)
Characterized by intense feeling (6)
Conduct; behavior; attitude (8)
Deep cleft in the ground; gorge (5)
Downward slope (9)
Excluded from a group (10)
Feel or express sorrow or regret (6)
Flowed out from; came from (8)
Gave up or put aside voluntarily (9)
Immoderately desirous of wealth; greedy (10)
Infect, inflame, or corrupt (6)
Injure or disfigure by removing or irreparably damaging parts (8)

Knowledge acquired by study; learning (9)
Make known; reveal; uncover (8)
Miserable; very unfortunate (8)
Money, food, or other donations given to the poor (4)
Of or belonging to old age or aged persons (6)
Person skilled in an applied art; craftsman (7)
Pious; religious; devoted to divine worship or service (6)
Pleasing to the taste and often temptingly served or delicate (6)
Respected (8)
Sacred or holy place; place of safety (9)
Temporary stay; brief period of residence (7)
Tendency to remain at rest or resist motion or change (7)
Things that are unimportant or frivolous (12)
Try hard (6)
Undeniably; unarguably (11)
Wise or judicious in practical affairs (7)
With overly-eager speed and possible carelessness (9)

Siddhartha Vocabulary Word Search 2 Answer Key

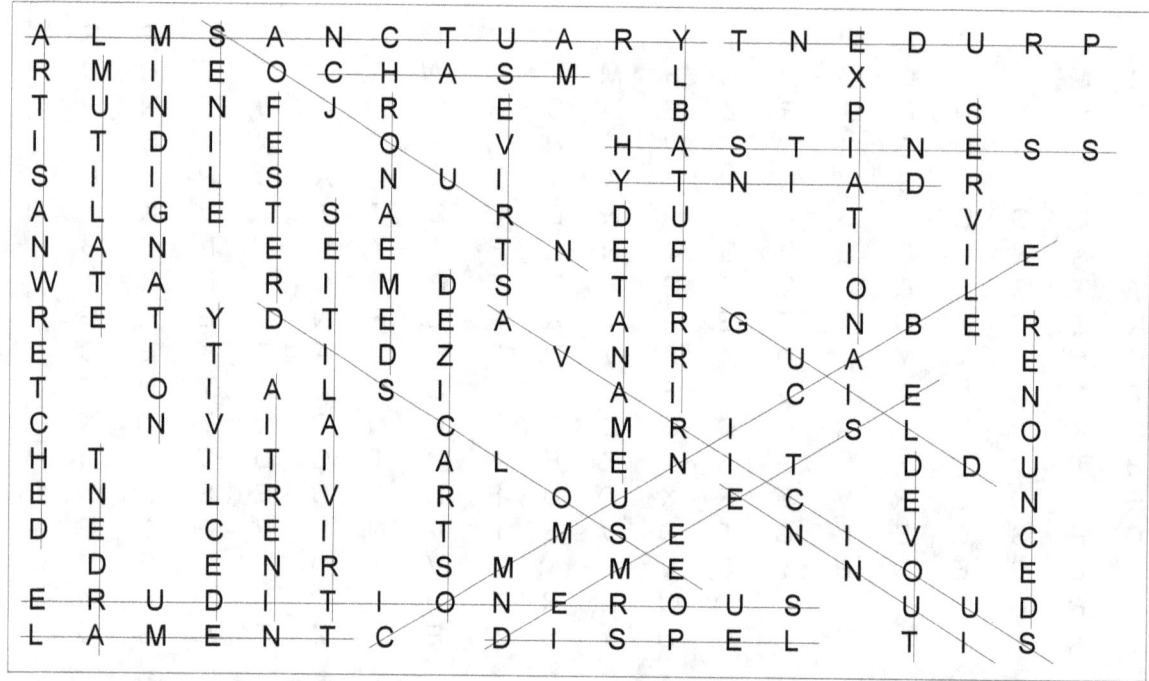

Act of atoning for sins or wrongdoing (9)
Anger aroused by something unjust, mean, or unworthy (11)
Association of tradesmen (5)
Boredom; dissatisfaction resulting from lack of interest (5)
Burdensome; oppressive; troublesome; causing hardship (7)
Capable of being easily communicated or transmitted (12)
Cause to vanish; get rid of (6)
Characteristic of, proper to, or customary for slaves (7)
Characterized by intense feeling (6)
Conduct; behavior; attitude (8)
Deep cleft in the ground; gorge (5)
Downward slope (9)
Excluded from a group (10)
Feel or express sorrow or regret (6)
Flowed out from; came from (8)
Gave up or put aside voluntarily (9)
Immoderately desirous of wealth; greedy (10)
Infect, inflame, or corrupt (6)
Injure or disfigure by removing or irreparably damaging parts (8)

Knowledge acquired by study; learning (9)
Make known; reveal; uncover (8)
Miserable; very unfortunate (8)
Money, food, or other donations given to the poor (4)
Of or belonging to old age or aged persons (6)
Person skilled in an applied art; craftsman (7)
Pious; religious; devoted to divine worship or service (6)
Pleasing to the taste and often temptingly served or delicate (6)
Respected (8)
Sacred or holy place; place of safety (9)
Temporary stay; brief period of residence (7)
Tendency to remain at rest or resist motion or change (7)
Things that are unimportant or frivolous (12)
Try hard (6)
Undeniably; unarguably (11)
Wise or judicious in practical affairs (7)
With overly-eager speed and possible carelessness (9)

Siddhartha Vocabulary Word Search 3

```
A O N E R O U S I W H I N D R A N C E W
V R M K G P V C N R A N O E O R L I L M
A F T R K P F I E S L I G N D A S I V D
R F S I B V W T R T F T R A E M N V P C
I E E M S N B E T C I Q A E E N E I R E
C S E S A A X C I H N C I M M T N R S N
I T S R T R N S A E E C P B E L T T S F
O E O P U E T A C D S O X U D P Z N V J
U E J Y C D R I M X S M E S Z K Z I P F
S M O F J E I D N V C M D A I N T Y R H
F E U S L G V T Y G Q U Z D D G B Z U P
L D R I V H I R I Q W N R X E S Y M D T
W S N K J B A M L O L I P R F T T M E K
A E T R W U L X U E N C P J I K U S N L
S U S R T X I D P T R A R V A Q O A T N
Z T S C I K T S S Q I B I K N L V H G D
D D N T E V I T A I L A P C X E C L L
F A M Y E D E W H W C E A S E X D I M D
S L S B Y R S X J E T T I T L V U T C M
E N N U I R E T D X P D Z F E G A L M S
```

ALMS	DISCLOSE	MUTILATE
ARDENT	DISPEL	ONEROUS
ARTISAN	ENNUI	PALLIATIVE
ASCETICS	ERUDITION	PRUDENT
AUSTERE	ESTEEMED	SANCTUARY
AVARICIOUS	EXPIATION	SENILE
CHASM	FESTER	SERVILE
COMMUNICABLE	GUILD	SMARTING
DAINTY	HASTINESS	SOJOURN
DECLIVITY	HINDRANCE	STRIVE
DEFIANCE	INERTIA	SUBMERGED
DEMEANOR	INTRINSIC	TRIVIALITIES
DEVOUT	LAMENT	WRETCHED

Siddhartha Vocabulary Word Search 3 Answer Key

ALMS	DISCLOSE	MUTILATE
ARDENT	DISPEL	ONEROUS
ARTISAN	ENNUI	PALLIATIVE
ASCETICS	ERUDITION	PRUDENT
AUSTERE	ESTEEMED	SANCTUARY
AVARICIOUS	EXPIATION	SENILE
CHASM	FESTER	SERVILE
COMMUNICABLE	GUILD	SMARTING
DAINTY	HASTINESS	SOJOURN
DECLIVITY	HINDRANCE	STRIVE
DEFIANCE	INERTIA	SUBMERGED
DEMEANOR	INTRINSIC	TRIVIALITIES
DEVOUT	LAMENT	WRETCHED

Siddhartha Vocabulary Word Search 4

```
A S C E T I C S I N S A T I A B L E D D
A R T I S A N S U B M E R G E D S Q V W
Q I R R E F U T A B L Y C S O J O U R N
I N T R I N S I C N Y R O T I S N A R T
S E N I L E D A I N T Y Y L A M E N T H
I N D I G N A T I O N D E C L I V I T Y
N O I T I D U R E L B A C I N U M M O C
H A S T I N E S S E I T I S R E V I D T
G S W I N C I P I E N T C W F E S T E R
A V A R I C I O U S A N C T U A R Y L Q
O F S T R I V E H A S S I D U O U S K L
D S Z X L P R E D E C E S S O R P P D H
C W T N E L O D N I D C F A I T R E N I
C O U R T E S A N D E V O U T E C O B N
E M A N A T E D H I M A R D E N T N P P
D E S O L C S I D S E G Z V U N M E C T
G U I L D H I R L P A K A O T U T R H K
A U S T E R E Z N E N Z N L S I Z O A J
N O I T A I P X E L O E V G M K M U S Q
D G M G G Q H I N D R A N C E S V S M H
```

ALMS	DISPEL	INSATIABLE
ARDENT	DIVERSITIES	INTRINSIC
ARTISAN	EMANATED	IRREFUTABLY
ASCETICS	ENNUI	LAMENT
ASSIDUOUS	EQUANIMITY	ONEROUS
AUSTERE	ERUDITION	OSTRACIZED
AVARICIOUS	EXPIATION	PREDECESSOR
CHASM	FESTER	RENOUNCED
COMMUNICABLE	GUILD	SANCTUARY
COURTESAN	HASTINESS	SENILE
DAINTY	HINDRANCE	SOJOURN
DECLIVITY	INCIPIENT	STRIVE
DEMEANOR	INDIGNATION	SUBMERGED
DEVOUT	INDOLENT	TRANSITORY
DISCLOSE	INERTIA	

Siddhartha Vocabulary Word Search 4 Answer Key

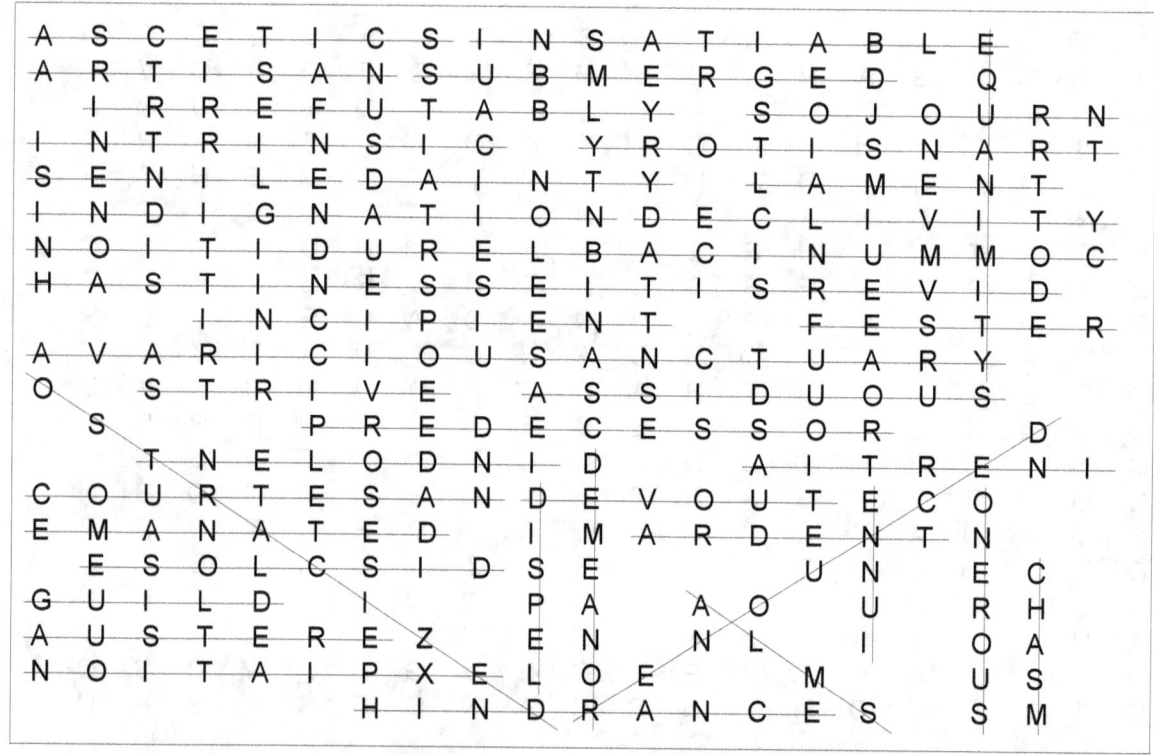

ALMS	DISPEL	INSATIABLE
ARDENT	DIVERSITIES	INTRINSIC
ARTISAN	EMANATED	IRREFUTABLY
ASCETICS	ENNUI	LAMENT
ASSIDUOUS	EQUANIMITY	ONEROUS
AUSTERE	ERUDITION	OSTRACIZED
AVARICIOUS	EXPIATION	PREDECESSOR
CHASM	FESTER	RENOUNCED
COMMUNICABLE	GUILD	SANCTUARY
COURTESAN	HASTINESS	SENILE
DAINTY	HINDRANCE	SOJOURN
DECLIVITY	INCIPIENT	STRIVE
DEMEANOR	INDIGNATION	SUBMERGED
DEVOUT	INDOLENT	TRANSITORY
DISCLOSE	INERTIA	

Siddhartha Vocabulary Crossword 1

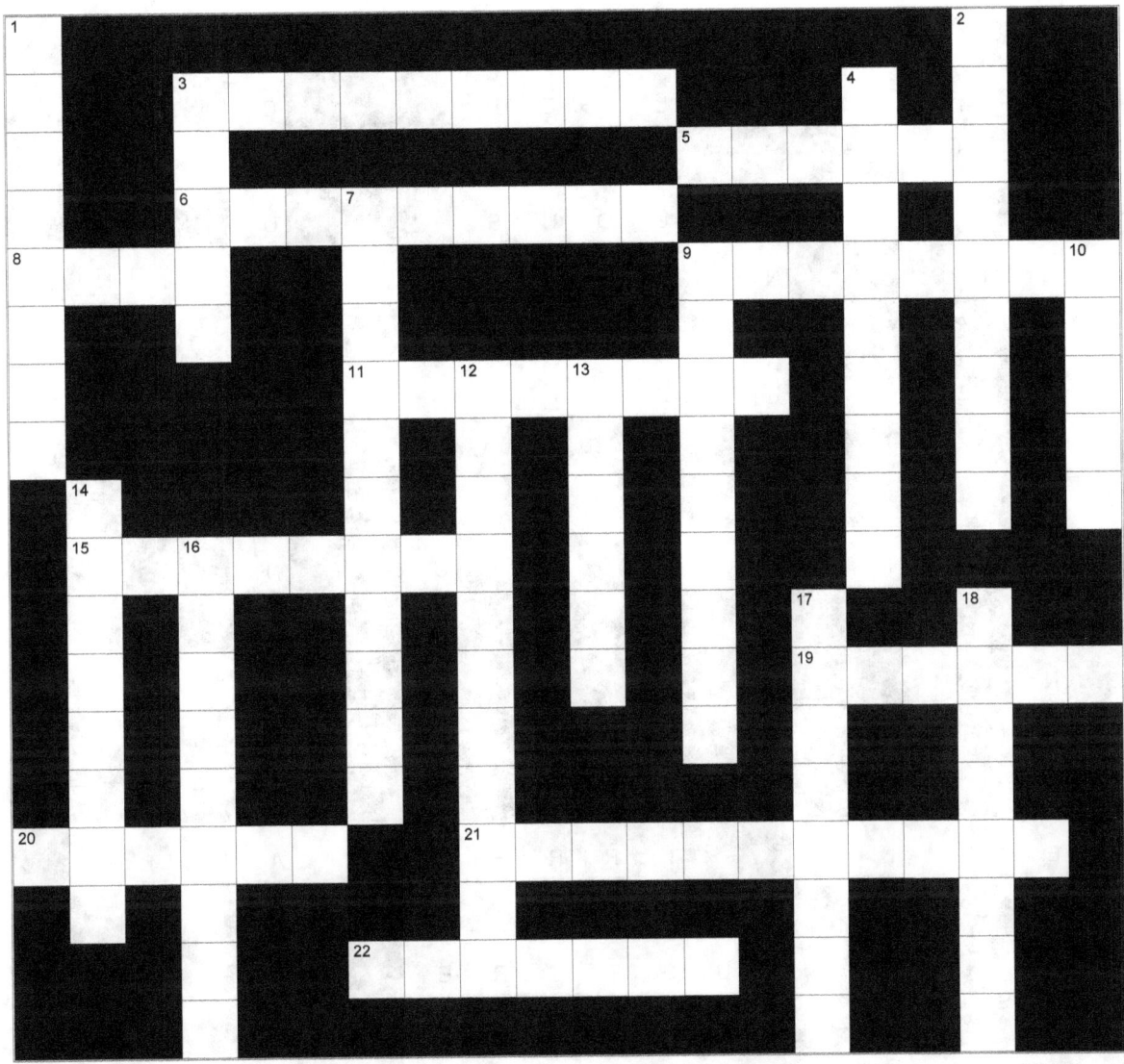

Across
3. Forced or driven to a course of action
5. Pious; religious; devoted to divine worship or service
6. Constant in effort; working diligently on a task
8. Money, food, or other donations given to the poor
9. Hurting with a sharp, usually superficial, stinging pain
11. Inactive; lethargic
15. Injure or disfigure by removing or irreparably damaging parts
19. Try hard
20. Of or belonging to old age or aged persons
21. Undeniably; unarguably
22. Severe in manner or appearance; strict

Down
1. Conduct; behavior; attitude
2. Belonging to a thing by its very nature
3. Deep cleft in the ground; gorge
4. Prostitute or paramour, esp. one associating with noblemen
7. Anger aroused by something unjust, mean, or unworthy
9. Sacred or holy place; place of safety
10. Association of tradesmen
12. Points or aspects in which things differ
13. Feel or express sorrow or regret
14. Flowed out from; came from
16. Persistent; stubborn
17. Those who renounce material comforts & lead a life of self-discipline
18. Make known; reveal; uncover

Siddhartha Vocabulary Crossword 1 Answer Key

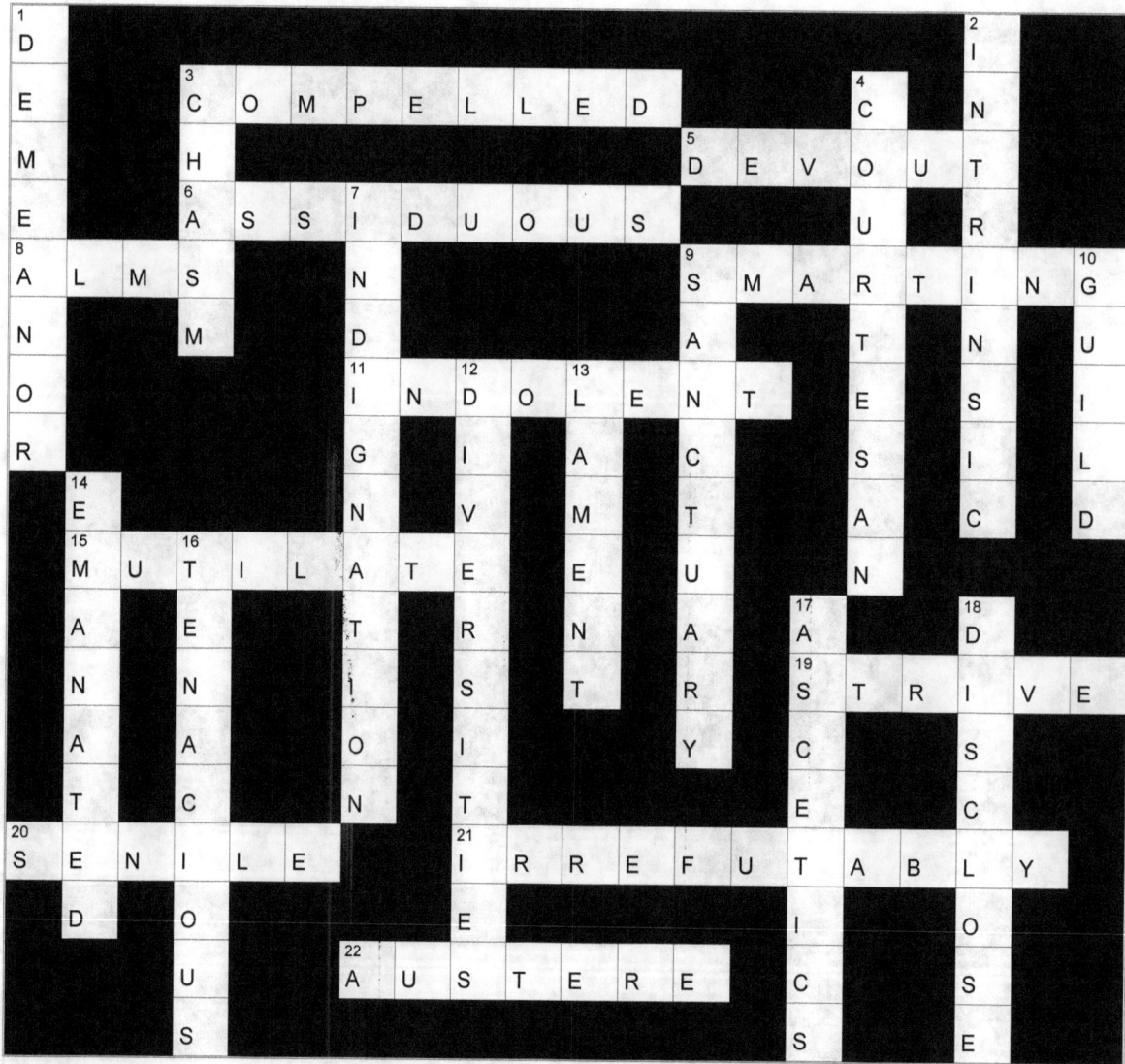

Across
- 3. Forced or driven to a course of action
- 5. Pious; religious; devoted to divine worship or service
- 6. Constant in effort; working diligently on a task
- 8. Money, food, or other donations given to the poor
- 9. Hurting with a sharp, usually superficial, stinging pain
- 11. Inactive; lethargic
- 15. Injure or disfigure by removing or irreparably damaging parts
- 19. Try hard
- 20. Of or belonging to old age or aged persons
- 21. Undeniably; unarguably
- 22. Severe in manner or appearance; strict

Down
- 1. Conduct; behavior; attitude
- 2. Belonging to a thing by its very nature
- 3. Deep cleft in the ground; gorge
- 4. Prostitute or paramour, esp. one associating with noblemen
- 7. Anger aroused by something unjust, mean, or unworthy
- 9. Sacred or holy place; place of safety
- 10. Association of tradesmen
- 12. Points or aspects in which things differ
- 13. Feel or express sorrow or regret
- 14. Flowed out from; came from
- 16. Persistent; stubborn
- 17. Those who renounce material comforts & lead a life of self-discipline
- 18. Make known; reveal; uncover

Siddhartha Vocabulary Crossword 2

Across
1. Money, food, or other donations given to the poor
3. Anger aroused by something unjust, mean, or unworthy
7. Conduct; behavior; attitude
8. Immoderately desirous of wealth; greedy
12. Characterized by intense feeling
13. Miserable; very unfortunate
15. Infect, inflame, or corrupt
17. Pious; religious; devoted to divine worship or service
20. Persistent; stubborn
21. Cause to vanish; get rid of
22. Beginning to exist or appear
23. Deep cleft in the ground; gorge

Down
2. Feel or express sorrow or regret
4. Association of tradesmen
5. Boredom; dissatisfaction resulting from lack of interest
6. Wise or judicious in practical affairs
8. Severe in manner or appearance; strict
9. Those who renounce material comforts & lead a life of self-discipline
10. Belonging to a thing by its very nature
11. Sacred or holy place; place of safety
14. Act of atoning for sins or wrongdoing
16. Gave up or put aside voluntarily
17. Points or aspects in which things differ
18. Excluded from a group
19. Person skilled in an applied art; craftsman

Siddhartha Vocabulary Crossword 2 Answer Key

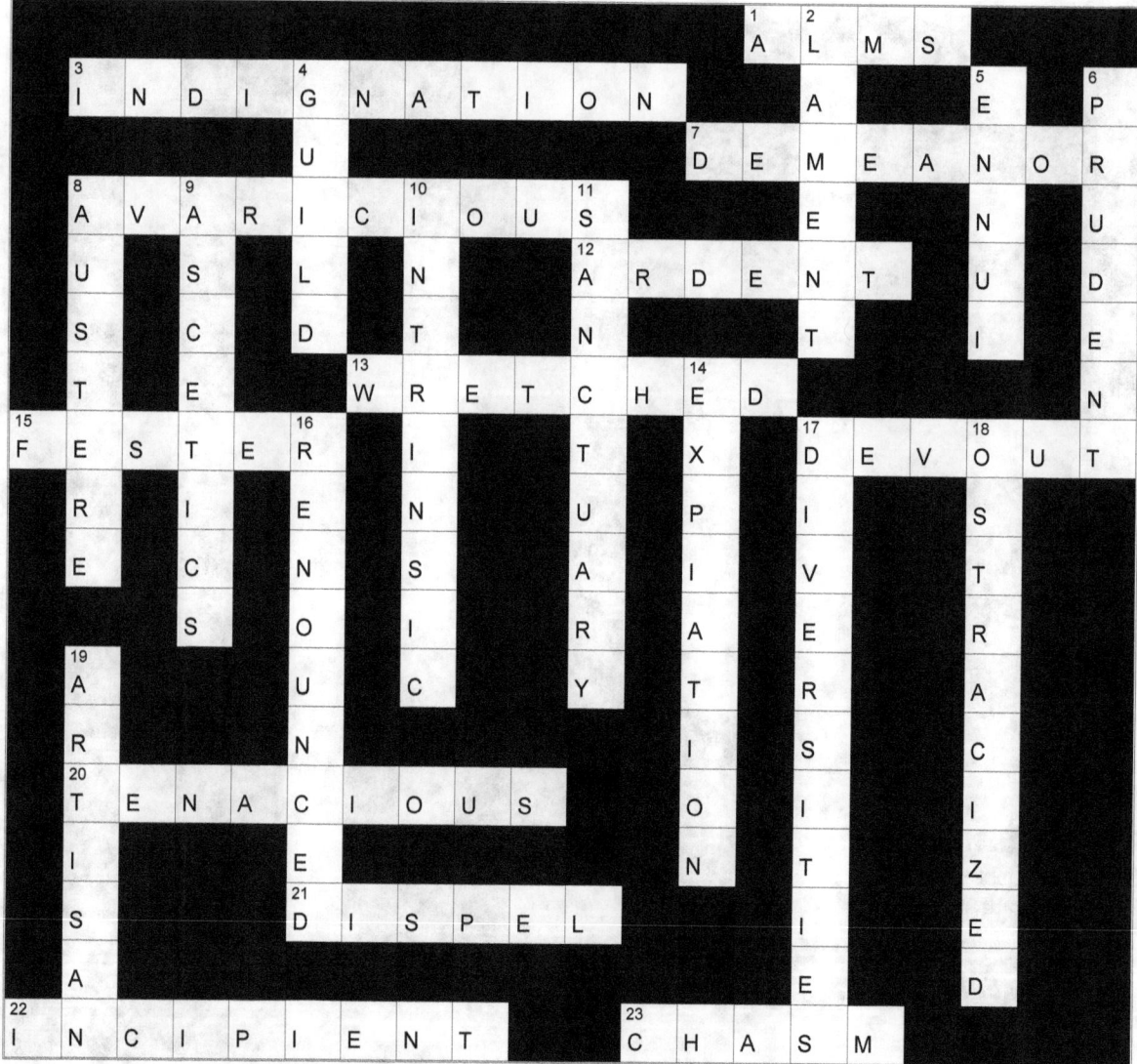

Across
1. Money, food, or other donations given to the poor
3. Anger aroused by something unjust, mean, or unworthy
7. Conduct; behavior; attitude
8. Immoderately desirous of wealth; greedy
12. Characterized by intense feeling
13. Miserable; very unfortunate
15. Infect, inflame, or corrupt
17. Pious; religious; devoted to divine worship or service
20. Persistent; stubborn
21. Cause to vanish; get rid of
22. Beginning to exist or appear
23. Deep cleft in the ground; gorge

Down
2. Feel or express sorrow or regret
4. Association of tradesmen
5. Boredom; dissatisfaction resulting from lack of interest
6. Wise or judicious in practical affairs
8. Severe in manner or appearance; strict
9. Those who renounce material comforts & lead a life of self-discipline
10. Belonging to a thing by its very nature
11. Sacred or holy place; place of safety
14. Act of atoning for sins or wrongdoing
16. Gave up or put aside voluntarily
17. Points or aspects in which things differ
18. Excluded from a group
19. Person skilled in an applied art; craftsman

Siddhartha Vocabulary Crossword 3

Across
1. Those who renounce material comforts & lead a life of self-discipline
3. Bold resistance to authority or any opposing force
7. Wise or judicious in practical affairs
9. Of or belonging to old age or aged persons
10. Can't be bothered, agitated, or upset
12. Immoderately desirous of wealth; greedy
17. Knowledge acquired by study; learning
18. Miserable; very unfortunate
19. Association of tradesmen
20. Feel or express sorrow or regret
22. Obstruction; something in the way or a burden
23. Quality of being calm and even-tempered; composure

Down
1. Characterized by intense feeling
2. Forced or driven to a course of action
4. Infect, inflame, or corrupt
5. Money, food, or other donations given to the poor
6. Conduct; behavior; attitude
8. Act of atoning for sins or wrongdoing
11. Points or aspects in which things differ
12. Severe in manner or appearance; strict
13. Belonging to a thing by its very nature
14. Sacred or holy place; place of safety
15. Injure or disfigure by removing or irreparably damaging parts
16. Downward slope
21. Deep cleft in the ground; gorge

Siddhartha Vocabulary Crossword 3 Answer Key

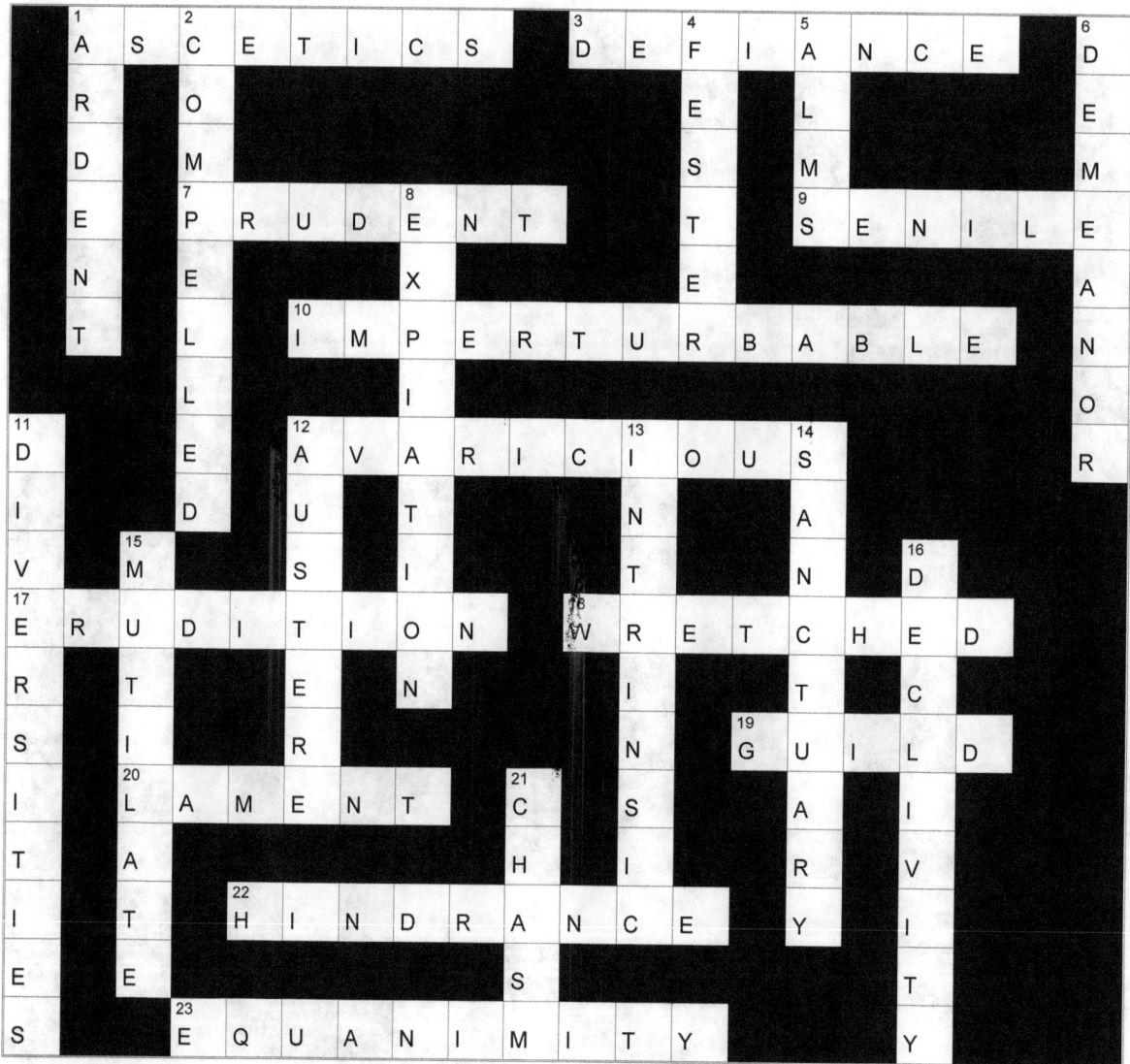

Across
1. Those who renounce material comforts & lead a life of self-discipline
3. Bold resistance to authority or any opposing force
7. Wise or judicious in practical affairs
9. Of or belonging to old age or aged persons
10. Can't be bothered, agitated, or upset
12. Immoderately desirous of wealth; greedy
17. Knowledge acquired by study; learning
18. Miserable; very unfortunate
19. Association of tradesmen
20. Feel or express sorrow or regret
22. Obstruction; something in the way or a burden
23. Quality of being calm and even-tempered; composure

Down
1. Characterized by intense feeling
2. Forced or driven to a course of action
4. Infect, inflame, or corrupt
5. Money, food, or other donations given to the poor
6. Conduct; behavior; attitude
8. Act of atoning for sins or wrongdoing
11. Points or aspects in which things differ
12. Severe in manner or appearance; strict
13. Belonging to a thing by its very nature
14. Sacred or holy place; place of safety
15. Injure or disfigure by removing or irreparably damaging parts
16. Downward slope
21. Deep cleft in the ground; gorge

Siddhartha Vocabulary Crossword 4

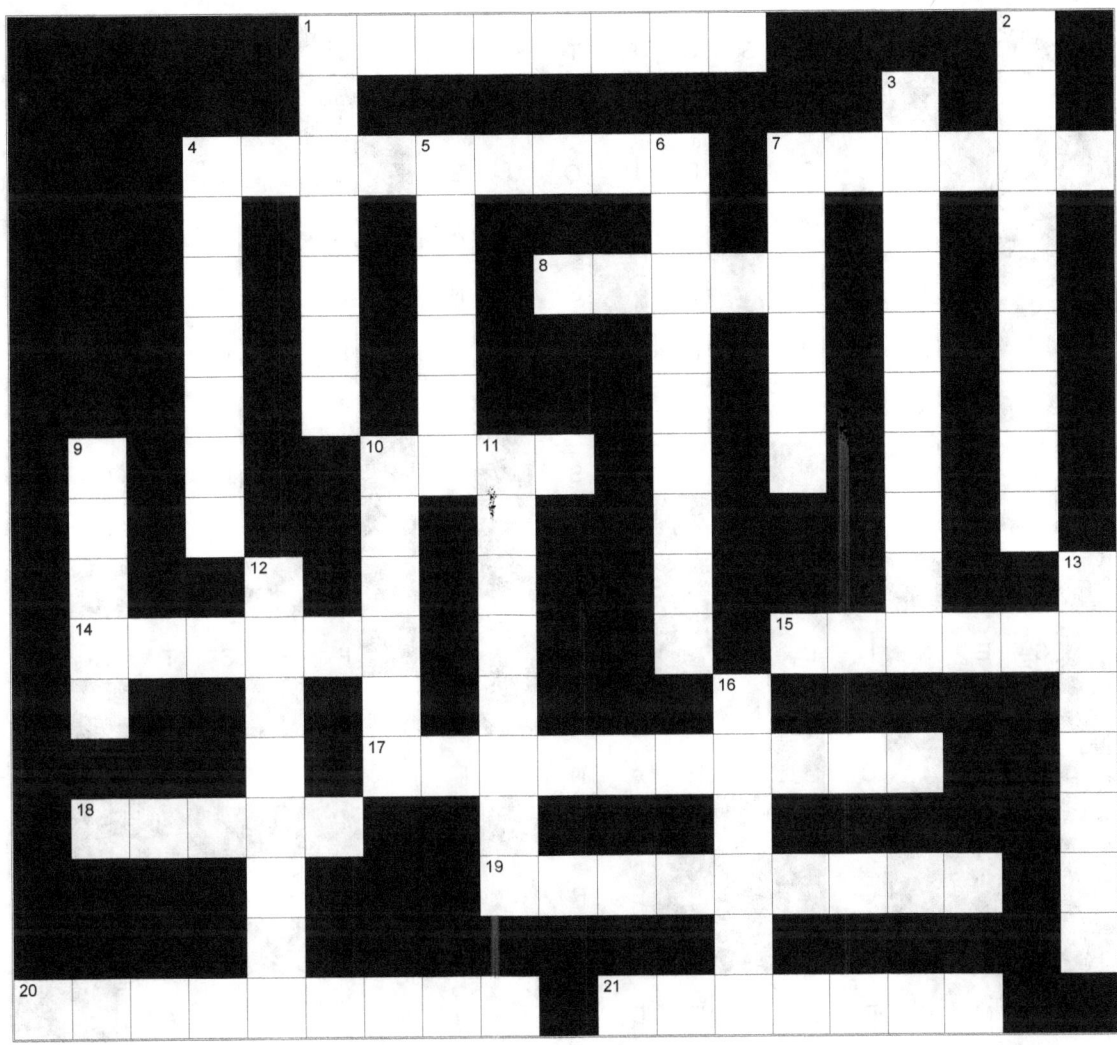

Across
1. Those who renounce material comforts & lead a life of self-discipline
4. Constant in effort; working diligently on a task
7. Pious; religious; devoted to divine worship or service
8. Boredom; dissatisfaction resulting from lack of interest
10. Money, food, or other donations given to the poor
14. Of or belonging to old age or aged persons
15. Infect, inflame, or corrupt
17. Not lasting, permanent, or eternal
18. Association of tradesmen
19. Knowledge acquired by study; learning
20. Forced or driven to a course of action
21. Tendency to remain at rest or resist motion or change

Down
1. Severe in manner or appearance; strict
2. Prostitute or paramour, esp. one associating with noblemen
3. Immoderately desirous of wealth; greedy
4. Person skilled in an applied art; craftsman
5. Cause to vanish; get rid of
6. Sacred or holy place; place of safety
7. Pleasing to the taste and often temptingly served or delicate
9. Deep cleft in the ground; gorge
10. Characterized by intense feeling
11. Injure or disfigure by removing or irreparably damaging parts
12. Make known; reveal; uncover
13. Wise or judicious in practical affairs
16. Try hard

Siddhartha Vocabulary Crossword 4 Answer Key

Across
1. Those who renounce material comforts & lead a life of self-discipline
4. Constant in effort; working diligently on a task
7. Pious; religious; devoted to divine worship or service
8. Boredom; dissatisfaction resulting from lack of interest
10. Money, food, or other donations given to the poor
14. Of or belonging to old age or aged persons
15. Infect, inflame, or corrupt
17. Not lasting, permanent, or eternal
18. Association of tradesmen
19. Knowledge acquired by study; learning
20. Forced or driven to a course of action
21. Tendency to remain at rest or resist motion or change

Down
1. Severe in manner or appearance; strict
2. Prostitute or paramour, esp. one associating with noblemen
3. Immoderately desirous of wealth; greedy
4. Person skilled in an applied art; craftsman
5. Cause to vanish; get rid of
6. Sacred or holy place; place of safety
7. Pleasing to the taste and often temptingly served or delicate
9. Deep cleft in the ground; gorge
10. Characterized by intense feeling
11. Injure or disfigure by removing or irreparably damaging parts
12. Make known; reveal; uncover
13. Wise or judicious in practical affairs
16. Try hard

ALMS	Money, food, or other donations given to the poor
ARDENT	Characterized by intense feeling
ARTISAN	Person skilled in an applied art; craftsman
ASCETICS	Those who renounce material comforts & lead a life of self-discipline
ASSIDUOUS	Constant in effort; working diligently on a task
AUSTERE	Severe in manner or appearance; strict

AVARICIOUS	Immoderately desirous of wealth; greedy
CHASM	Deep cleft in the ground; gorge
COMMUNICABLE	Capable of being easily communicated or transmitted
COMPELLED	Forced or driven to a course of action
CONSIDERATION	Thoughtful or sympathetic regard or respect
COURTESAN	Prostitute or paramour, esp. one associating with noblemen

DAINTY	Pleasing to the taste and often temptingly served or delicate
DECLIVITY	Downward slope
DEFIANCE	Bold resistance to authority or any opposing force
DEMEANOR	Conduct; behavior; attitude
DEVOUT	Pious; religious; devoted to divine worship or service
DISCLOSE	Make known; reveal; uncover

DISILLUSIONMENT	State of being freed from false beliefs
DISPEL	Cause to vanish; get rid of
DIVERSITIES	Points or aspects in which things differ
EMANATED	Flowed out from; came from
ENNUI	Boredom; dissatisfaction resulting from lack of interest
EQUANIMITY	Quality of being calm and even-tempered; composure

ERUDITION	Knowledge acquired by study; learning
ESTEEMED	Respected
EXPIATION	Act of atoning for sins or wrongdoing
FESTER	Infect, inflame, or corrupt
GUILD	Association of tradesmen
HASTINESS	With overly-eager speed and possible carelessness

HINDRANCE	Obstruction; something in the way or a burden
IMPERTURBABLE	Can't be bothered, agitated, or upset
INCIPIENT	Beginning to exist or appear
INDIGNATION	Anger aroused by something unjust, mean, or unworthy
INDOLENT	Inactive; lethargic
INERTIA	Tendency to remain at rest or resist motion or change

INSATIABLE	Incapable of being satisfied or appeased
INTRINSIC	Belonging to a thing by its very nature
IRREFUTABLY	Undeniably; unarguably
LAMENT	Feel or express sorrow or regret
MUTILATE	Injure or disfigure by removing or irreparably damaging parts
ONEROUS	Burdensome; oppressive; troublesome; causing hardship

OSTRACIZED	Excluded from a group
PALLIATIVE	Something that makes pain or sorrow easier to bear
PREDECESSOR	One who came before another in holding an office or position
PRUDENT	Wise or judicious in practical affairs
RENOUNCED	Gave up or put aside voluntarily
SANCTUARY	Sacred or holy place; place of safety

SENILE	Of or belonging to old age or aged persons
SERVILE	Characteristic of, proper to, or customary for slaves
SMARTING	Hurting with a sharp, usually superficial, stinging pain
SOJOURN	Temporary stay; brief period of residence
STRIVE	Try hard
SUBMERGED	Sunk below the surface

TENACIOUS	Persistent; stubborn
TRANSITORY	Not lasting, permanent, or eternal
TRIVIALITIES	Things that are unimportant or frivolous
VENERABLENESS	Quality of commanding respect by virtue of age, character, or position
WRETCHED	Miserable; very unfortunate

Siddhartha Vocabulary

COURTESAN	INCIPIENT	INERTIA	ASCETICS	AUSTERE
SMARTING	DISCLOSE	DISPEL	ONEROUS	EQUANIMITY
FESTER	ERUDITION	FREE SPACE	OSTRACIZED	IMPERTURBABLE
EXPIATION	RENOUNCED	COMPELLED	PREDECESSOR	STRIVE
SOJOURN	LAMENT	TRIVIALITIES	DEVOUT	DEFIANCE

Siddhartha Vocabulary

CONSIDERATION	WRETCHED	INDOLENT	ALMS	INTRINSIC
TRANSITORY	MUTILATE	SENILE	SERVILE	PALLIATIVE
HINDRANCE	GUILD	FREE SPACE	EMANATED	ESTEEMED
DAINTY	PRUDENT	COMMUNICABLE	ARTISAN	HASTINESS
DEMEANOR	TENACIOUS	AVARICIOUS	IRREFUTABLY	VENERABLENESS

Siddhartha Vocabulary

INDOLENT	WRETCHED	ESTEEMED	INERTIA	ENNUI
INSATIABLE	FESTER	DIVERSITIES	GUILD	COMPELLED
SANCTUARY	ARTISAN	FREE SPACE	SENILE	HINDRANCE
PRUDENT	EMANATED	CONSIDERATION	AUSTERE	SOJOURN
DEFIANCE	DISCLOSE	DECLIVITY	CHASM	ASCETICS

Siddhartha Vocabulary

IMPERTURBABLE	ONEROUS	ALMS	VENERABLENESS	DISILLUSIONMENT
DEVOUT	SERVILE	MUTILATE	PALLIATIVE	LAMENT
HASTINESS	COURTESAN	FREE SPACE	DEMEANOR	ARDENT
TRIVIALITIES	AVARICIOUS	INCIPIENT	COMMUNICABLE	DISPEL
DAINTY	PREDECESSOR	ASSIDUOUS	TENACIOUS	SUBMERGED

Siddhartha Vocabulary

INDOLENT	ALMS	PREDECESSOR	DEFIANCE	ASSIDUOUS
IMPERTURBABLE	PALLIATIVE	DECLIVITY	EXPIATION	INCIPIENT
SANCTUARY	RENOUNCED	FREE SPACE	COMMUNICABLE	WRETCHED
GUILD	ERUDITION	VENERABLENESS	TRANSITORY	EQUANIMITY
MUTILATE	CONSIDERATION	DAINTY	INSATIABLE	STRIVE

Siddhartha Vocabulary

ARTISAN	DISPEL	EMANATED	SERVILE	AVARICIOUS
SUBMERGED	COURTESAN	PRUDENT	DEVOUT	HINDRANCE
OSTRACIZED	ENNUI	FREE SPACE	LAMENT	COMPELLED
SENILE	FESTER	INTRINSIC	SOJOURN	DISCLOSE
DIVERSITIES	TRIVIALITIES	CHASM	SMARTING	TENACIOUS

Siddhartha Vocabulary

INDOLENT	EXPIATION	LAMENT	EMANATED	SERVILE
EQUANIMITY	VENERABLENESS	INTRINSIC	INERTIA	CONSIDERATION
COURTESAN	SENILE	FREE SPACE	DEFIANCE	ASCETICS
RENOUNCED	TRANSITORY	DEVOUT	PREDECESSOR	PRUDENT
COMPELLED	ALMS	ARDENT	DEMEANOR	HASTINESS

Siddhartha Vocabulary

SOJOURN	WRETCHED	ARTISAN	INSATIABLE	DISILLUSIONMENT
FESTER	SMARTING	IRREFUTABLY	AVARICIOUS	ONEROUS
ENNUI	OSTRACIZED	FREE SPACE	GUILD	INDIGNATION
ASSIDUOUS	PALLIATIVE	DAINTY	AUSTERE	DISPEL
SANCTUARY	ERUDITION	IMPERTURBABLE	TRIVIALITIES	DECLIVITY

Siddhartha Vocabulary

DAINTY	IRREFUTABLY	AVARICIOUS	HASTINESS	GUILD
INERTIA	ARTISAN	TENACIOUS	SOJOURN	RENOUNCED
ALMS	SMARTING	FREE SPACE	SERVILE	ENNUI
EQUANIMITY	FESTER	EMANATED	INTRINSIC	DISILLUSIONMENT
WRETCHED	DEVOUT	HINDRANCE	DEFIANCE	OSTRACIZED

Siddhartha Vocabulary

INDOLENT	DISCLOSE	EXPIATION	PALLIATIVE	ASCETICS
PREDECESSOR	PRUDENT	VENERABLENESS	ESTEEMED	ERUDITION
DECLIVITY	LAMENT	FREE SPACE	SANCTUARY	STRIVE
INCIPIENT	MUTILATE	CONSIDERATION	AUSTERE	COMPELLED
ASSIDUOUS	COURTESAN	CHASM	COMMUNICABLE	DIVERSITIES

Siddhartha Vocabulary

PALLIATIVE	SOJOURN	AVARICIOUS	TRIVIALITIES	EXPIATION
COURTESAN	RENOUNCED	EMANATED	DECLIVITY	SUBMERGED
INSATIABLE	DIVERSITIES	FREE SPACE	EQUANIMITY	INCIPIENT
COMMUNICABLE	LAMENT	SANCTUARY	INERTIA	ESTEEMED
ASCETICS	OSTRACIZED	INDIGNATION	ASSIDUOUS	FESTER

Siddhartha Vocabulary

ERUDITION	HASTINESS	IMPERTURBABLE	PRUDENT	ARDENT
DAINTY	GUILD	SMARTING	MUTILATE	AUSTERE
DISILLUSIONMENT	ONEROUS	FREE SPACE	STRIVE	DEFIANCE
INTRINSIC	PREDECESSOR	HINDRANCE	TENACIOUS	SERVILE
INDOLENT	SENILE	CHASM	DEMEANOR	ENNUI

Siddhartha Vocabulary

SENILE	LAMENT	ESTEEMED	ERUDITION	ARTISAN
CONSIDERATION	DISILLUSIONMENT	IMPERTURBABLE	INCIPIENT	COURTESAN
DEVOUT	TRANSITORY	FREE SPACE	ALMS	DISCLOSE
TRIVIALITIES	INSATIABLE	INTRINSIC	EXPIATION	VENERABLENESS
INDOLENT	ARDENT	DEMEANOR	GUILD	SMARTING

Siddhartha Vocabulary

STRIVE	PREDECESSOR	EQUANIMITY	HASTINESS	DEFIANCE
DAINTY	FESTER	ENNUI	SANCTUARY	INDIGNATION
DIVERSITIES	HINDRANCE	FREE SPACE	SOJOURN	ASCETICS
DISPEL	CHASM	MUTILATE	PALLIATIVE	OSTRACIZED
PRUDENT	TENACIOUS	IRREFUTABLY	ONEROUS	DECLIVITY

Siddhartha Vocabulary

ALMS	LAMENT	ASCETICS	RENOUNCED	ONEROUS
DEMEANOR	GUILD	CONSIDERATION	DEFIANCE	SANCTUARY
IMPERTURBABLE	ARDENT	FREE SPACE	TRIVIALITIES	INDOLENT
HINDRANCE	DAINTY	INCIPIENT	AVARICIOUS	SERVILE
WRETCHED	SUBMERGED	DISPEL	SMARTING	STRIVE

Siddhartha Vocabulary

DISCLOSE	DIVERSITIES	ARTISAN	CHASM	EMANATED
AUSTERE	MUTILATE	ASSIDUOUS	EQUANIMITY	COMMUNICABLE
INTRINSIC	COMPELLED	FREE SPACE	COURTESAN	SOJOURN
INERTIA	HASTINESS	TRANSITORY	OSTRACIZED	ERUDITION
ENNUI	PREDECESSOR	DECLIVITY	DISILLUSIONMENT	INDIGNATION

Siddhartha Vocabulary

SUBMERGED	PREDECESSOR	WRETCHED	PRUDENT	FESTER
EXPIATION	INTRINSIC	COMMUNICABLE	DIVERSITIES	DEMEANOR
MUTILATE	IRREFUTABLY	FREE SPACE	IMPERTURBABLE	ESTEEMED
DAINTY	ALMS	DISILLUSIONMENT	SANCTUARY	INDIGNATION
VENERABLENESS	ARDENT	INSATIABLE	DISCLOSE	EMANATED

Siddhartha Vocabulary

AVARICIOUS	TRANSITORY	TRIVIALITIES	GUILD	INDOLENT
SMARTING	RENOUNCED	AUSTERE	DEVOUT	TENACIOUS
SOJOURN	COMPELLED	FREE SPACE	ARTISAN	ASSIDUOUS
SERVILE	CHASM	OSTRACIZED	ENNUI	ASCETICS
HINDRANCE	DECLIVITY	CONSIDERATION	INERTIA	COURTESAN

Siddhartha Vocabulary

INSATIABLE	RENOUNCED	DISCLOSE	ERUDITION	INERTIA
ARTISAN	SERVILE	EXPIATION	TRANSITORY	TRIVIALITIES
MUTILATE	SOJOURN	FREE SPACE	INCIPIENT	SMARTING
TENACIOUS	SANCTUARY	DEMEANOR	STRIVE	IRREFUTABLY
ALMS	DIVERSITIES	GUILD	ASCETICS	ASSIDUOUS

Siddhartha Vocabulary

VENERABLENESS	OSTRACIZED	HINDRANCE	DISILLUSIONMENT	CONSIDERATION
EMANATED	IMPERTURBABLE	INDIGNATION	WRETCHED	PRUDENT
COMPELLED	INDOLENT	FREE SPACE	EQUANIMITY	DECLIVITY
COURTESAN	PALLIATIVE	PREDECESSOR	AVARICIOUS	HASTINESS
DEFIANCE	ESTEEMED	DEVOUT	ARDENT	FESTER

Siddhartha Vocabulary

DEFIANCE	DISILLUSIONMENT	INSATIABLE	PREDECESSOR	SANCTUARY
SMARTING	LAMENT	GUILD	IMPERTURBABLE	ALMS
PALLIATIVE	DIVERSITIES	FREE SPACE	ESTEEMED	COMMUNICABLE
ENNUI	VENERABLENESS	DAINTY	EQUANIMITY	HINDRANCE
TRANSITORY	ARTISAN	EMANATED	AUSTERE	DEVOUT

Siddhartha Vocabulary

SERVILE	HASTINESS	ERUDITION	INDOLENT	ASSIDUOUS
STRIVE	ONEROUS	OSTRACIZED	CHASM	INERTIA
ASCETICS	ARDENT	FREE SPACE	DEMEANOR	DISPEL
EXPIATION	TRIVIALITIES	SENILE	CONSIDERATION	MUTILATE
DECLIVITY	IRREFUTABLY	INTRINSIC	PRUDENT	TENACIOUS

Siddhartha Vocabulary

AUSTERE	HASTINESS	OSTRACIZED	TRIVIALITIES	TRANSITORY
RENOUNCED	SMARTING	MUTILATE	IMPERTURBABLE	LAMENT
EMANATED	DIVERSITIES	FREE SPACE	CONSIDERATION	ONEROUS
PALLIATIVE	ARTISAN	INSATIABLE	VENERABLENESS	INERTIA
ESTEEMED	INCIPIENT	DECLIVITY	INDIGNATION	ENNUI

Siddhartha Vocabulary

GUILD	DEVOUT	PREDECESSOR	CHASM	DISILLUSIONMENT
ASCETICS	PRUDENT	INTRINSIC	ASSIDUOUS	STRIVE
COURTESAN	DISPEL	FREE SPACE	SERVILE	HINDRANCE
INDOLENT	EQUANIMITY	ERUDITION	DAINTY	COMPELLED
SUBMERGED	TENACIOUS	SENILE	COMMUNICABLE	IRREFUTABLY

Siddhartha Vocabulary

SOJOURN	DIVERSITIES	GUILD	LAMENT	COMMUNICABLE
ONEROUS	ESTEEMED	DAINTY	IRREFUTABLY	ENNUI
PRUDENT	DEMEANOR	FREE SPACE	SUBMERGED	DISCLOSE
INTRINSIC	ASSIDUOUS	STRIVE	OSTRACIZED	COMPELLED
PREDECESSOR	FESTER	IMPERTURBABLE	ERUDITION	EMANATED

Siddhartha Vocabulary

DEFIANCE	ARTISAN	TENACIOUS	DISILLUSIONMENT	ALMS
ASCETICS	SENILE	DEVOUT	ARDENT	INDOLENT
VENERABLENESS	CHASM	FREE SPACE	SMARTING	WRETCHED
INERTIA	TRANSITORY	TRIVIALITIES	INSATIABLE	PALLIATIVE
INDIGNATION	HINDRANCE	AUSTERE	SANCTUARY	EQUANIMITY

Siddhartha Vocabulary

DISPEL	TENACIOUS	DISCLOSE	RENOUNCED	DAINTY
DECLIVITY	ARDENT	SMARTING	AVARICIOUS	INDOLENT
SANCTUARY	TRIVIALITIES	FREE SPACE	ERUDITION	PREDECESSOR
FESTER	ASCETICS	INTRINSIC	COURTESAN	HASTINESS
MUTILATE	DISILLUSIONMENT	SUBMERGED	PALLIATIVE	STRIVE

Siddhartha Vocabulary

ENNUI	COMPELLED	TRANSITORY	OSTRACIZED	WRETCHED
EQUANIMITY	DEMEANOR	EXPIATION	VENERABLENESS	SOJOURN
ESTEEMED	AUSTERE	FREE SPACE	ALMS	INSATIABLE
INERTIA	SERVILE	DEVOUT	ARTISAN	INDIGNATION
EMANATED	CONSIDERATION	LAMENT	ASSIDUOUS	GUILD

Siddhartha Vocabulary

TRANSITORY	VENERABLENESS	EMANATED	INERTIA	CONSIDERATION
ONEROUS	CHASM	GUILD	PALLIATIVE	DAINTY
OSTRACIZED	DEVOUT	FREE SPACE	DECLIVITY	INSATIABLE
DISILLUSIONMENT	EQUANIMITY	STRIVE	ARTISAN	ARDENT
WRETCHED	SANCTUARY	INCIPIENT	PREDECESSOR	INDIGNATION

Siddhartha Vocabulary

AUSTERE	INDOLENT	DIVERSITIES	LAMENT	ENNUI
IMPERTURBABLE	SUBMERGED	RENOUNCED	COURTESAN	MUTILATE
AVARICIOUS	COMPELLED	FREE SPACE	DISCLOSE	DEMEANOR
COMMUNICABLE	HASTINESS	ASSIDUOUS	SENILE	DISPEL
INTRINSIC	HINDRANCE	DEFIANCE	PRUDENT	ASCETICS

Siddhartha Vocabulary

MUTILATE	PRUDENT	INDOLENT	ASCETICS	EQUANIMITY
INDIGNATION	STRIVE	INSATIABLE	GUILD	ESTEEMED
DEFIANCE	ONEROUS	FREE SPACE	AVARICIOUS	FESTER
SOJOURN	TRIVIALITIES	ERUDITION	PALLIATIVE	TENACIOUS
DISCLOSE	INERTIA	EMANATED	ARTISAN	AUSTERE

Siddhartha Vocabulary

SANCTUARY	SMARTING	IMPERTURBABLE	DEMEANOR	ARDENT
DIVERSITIES	TRANSITORY	DECLIVITY	COMMUNICABLE	SERVILE
COURTESAN	HASTINESS	FREE SPACE	CONSIDERATION	ALMS
WRETCHED	HINDRANCE	RENOUNCED	SUBMERGED	INCIPIENT
DEVOUT	VENERABLENESS	PREDECESSOR	CHASM	INTRINSIC

www.ingramcontent.com/pod-product-compliance
Lightning Source LLC
Chambersburg PA
CBHW081454070526
44586CB00019B/2354